❦ ROBERT FROST: AN INTRODUCTION

ROBERT FROST
AN INTRODUCTION

edited by
Robert A. Greenberg
and
James G. Hepburn

HOLT, RINEHART AND WINSTON, INC.
NEW YORK

cover design by Margaret D. Hepburn

☙ FOREWORD

When Robert Frost wrote that "the fact is the sweetest dream that labor knows," he affirmed a possibility. So it is with this pamphlet. The facts are here. Each poem, review, and article is a fact. There are facts from which to create facts: information and evidence to be discovered, selected, marshaled, and presented in a new form. There are opportunities for learning facts about footnoting and bibliography. In the process, the student may transform his investigation into an imaginative experience. Frost's poems will help, and so will the criticism.

To Amy Lowell, Frost's poetry is a simple, solemn photograph of New England; to William Rose Benét, it is the earthy, wise, and artful expression of a great man; to Lionel Trilling, it is a vision of a terrifying universe. These opposed views indicate some of the general matters with which this pamphlet is concerned: the relationship of a poem to the poet and to the world; the nature of a poem and the art of it. The opening material in the pamphlet is relatively simple: the three comments on "After Apple-Picking" merely suggest ways in which the poem can be approached, and the student should have little difficulty in grasping their substance—and perhaps only a little more difficulty in distinguishing the approaches as they could be applied to any poem. The material becomes progressively more difficult, but almost none of it presupposes special literary interests or understanding.

Many of the selections are offered complete as they originally appeared. Original pagination is provided for all the material. Some of the research topics given in the appendix are designed so that the teacher can—if he wishes—require the student to consult the library for specific additional sources for individual topics.

February, 1961   ROBERT A. GREENBERG

                                                        JAMES G. HEPBURN

ꙮ CONTENTS

❦ ROBERT FROST: A BIOGRAPHICAL NOTE

Robert Frost was born on March 26, 1874, in San Francisco, where his father, of firm New Hampshire stock, edited a newspaper. The paper was Democratic and Robert's full name is Robert Lee Frost, two facts which are usually taken to indicate the elder Frost's attitude to then-Republican New England. When Robert was eleven, his father died, and he and his schoolteacher mother crossed country and settled with relatives in Massachusetts. His first published poem, on the subject of Cortez in Mexico, appeared in the high school newspaper when he was sixteen. He entered Dartmouth at the age of eighteen, but remained for only about seven weeks. Two years later, in 1895, he married Elinor White, whom he had known in high school. In 1897 he enrolled at Harvard, hoping to prepare for a career in college teaching, but he left after two years without a degree. Frost was then twenty-five.

Disappointed with Frost's erratic progress, his grandfather presented him with a farm in Derry, New Hampshire, on the condition that he retain it for ten years. Farming proved less than profitable, and Frost supplemented his income by teaching school, first at the Pinkerton Academy in Derry and then for a year at the New Hampshire State Normal School in Plymouth, where he taught psychology. Throughout this time he was writing poetry, and though he offered it to various periodicals, very little was printed. When his ten-year obligation at the farm ended, Frost sold the property, and shortly after, in September 1912, he and his family left for England. There he met a number of expatriate American poets, most notably Ezra Pound, but he felt greatest affinity with a group of English poets—Edward Thomas, Lascelles Abercrombie, Wilfred Gibson—who often wrote of rural subjects. Frost's first book of poetry, *A Boy's Will*, consisting largely of what he had written prior to coming to England, was issued in 1913 by an English publisher, who a year later issued Frost's second volume, *North of Boston.* Frost returned to America in 1915 to discover that an American edition of *North of Boston* had recently appeared and that it had provoked a highly favorable response. Later that year *A Boy's Will* also appeared in an American edition.

From this time on, Frost's status as a notable American poet was secure. Though he settled for a time in New Hampshire, and then more permanently in Vermont, he traveled throughout much of the country giving lectures and public readings from his own poetry. His earlier lack of success at Dartmouth and Harvard was more than compensated for by his stints as poet-in-residence at such colleges and universities as Amherst, Harvard, Michigan, and Dartmouth. And he continued to write: in 1916, *Mountain Interval;* in 1923, *New Hampshire;* in 1928, *West-running Brook;* in 1936, *A Further Range;* in 1942, *A Witness Tree;* in 1945, *A Masque of Reason;* in 1947, *Steeple Bush* and *A Masque of Mercy.* His public honors have been many: four Pulitzer Prizes for Poetry (1924, 1931, 1937, 1943), innumerable honorary degrees (including ones from Oxford and Cambridge), membership in the National Institute of Arts and Letters (1916) and in the American Academy (1930), the Mark Twain Medal (1937) and the Emerson-Thoreau Medal (1958), the office of Consultant in Poetry to the Library of Congress (1958-1959), and formal felicitations from the United States Senate on his seventy-fifth birthday and then again on his eighty-fifth birthday.

❦ ROBERT FROST: AN INTRODUCTION

❦ THREE POEMS
❦ WITH COMMENTARIES

❦❦❦❦❦❦❦❦❦❦❦❦❦❦❦❦❦❦❦

After Apple-Picking

My long two-pointed ladder's sticking through a tree
Toward heaven still,
And there's a barrel that I didn't fill
Beside it, and there may be two or three
Apples I didn't pick upon some bough.
But I am done with apple-picking now.
Essence of winter sleep is on the night,
The scent of apples: I am drowsing off.
I cannot rub the strangeness from my sight
I got from looking through a pane of glass
I skimmed this morning from the drinking trough
And held against the world of hoary grass.
It melted, and I let it fall and break.
But I was well
Upon my way to sleep before it fell,
And I could tell
What form my dreaming was about to take.
Magnified apples appear and disappear,
Stem end and blossom end,
And every fleck of russet showing clear.
My instep arch not only keeps the ache,
It keeps the pressure of a ladder-round.
I feel the ladder sway as the boughs bend.
And I keep hearing from the cellar bin
The rumbling sound
Of load on load of apples coming in.
For I have had too much
Of apple-picking: I am overtired

Of the great harvest I myself desired.
There were ten thousand thousand fruit to touch,
Cherish in hand, lift down, and not let fall.
For all
That struck the earth,
No matter if not bruised or spiked with stubble,
Went surely to the cider-apple heap
As of no worth.
One can see what will trouble
This sleep of mine, whatever sleep it is.
Were he not gone,
The woodchuck could say whether it's like his
Long sleep, as I describe its coming on,
Or just some human sleep.

ẃ LOUIS UNTERMEYER[1]

"After Apple-Picking" is so vivid a memory of experience
that the reader absorbs it physically. He smells the heady scent
of apples; senses the strangeness of the world as it seems to the
overtired worker; feels how definitely the instep arch

> . . . not only keeps the ache,
> It keeps the pressure of a ladder-round.

It is all so simple and exact, so casual yet so original. A poem
of reality, "After Apple-Picking" has the enchantment of a
lingering dream. [244]

ẃ ELIZABETH SHEPLEY SERGEANT[2]

Some have thought that "After Apple-Picking" derived in
its richness from the rich tended orchards of Herefordshire, a
true cider country, where Carol [Frost's son], the tall stripling

---

[1] From *The Road Not Taken*, New York: Holt, 1951, p. 244.
[2] From *Robert Frost: The Trial by Existence*, New York: Holt,
Rinehart and Winston, 1960, pp. 118-119.

with his father's eyes and charming smile, loved to sort and wrap superlative English fruit for market. In fact, the manuscript had been surrendered before the move, and the supremely fine [118] ode on apples and trancelike sleep—which perfects the form used in "My Butterfly" and "Storm Fear"—grew out of the unpruned, unsprayed meager orchards of Derry. In Frost's *North of Boston,* "The Wood-Pile," "The Mountain," and "After Apple-Picking," all three largely written, he told me, before he went to England, stand as landmarks of habitual attention and action to New England folks staring into dark abysses or shrewdly counting their blessings. All these Yankees had climbed their mountains to drink at a spring, had built their wood piles and gone drowsy with their apple-picking. [119]

CLEANTH BROOKS[3]

In the more ambitious poems Frost's central problem is to develop depth of feeling without seeming to violate the realistic and matter of fact elements of the situation with which the poem deals.

His successful poems are thus successes in the handling of tone. Some of Frost's admirers, in insisting on the poet as a sort of kindly homespun philosopher, neglect the far more important matter: that popular poetry of this sort usually becomes pretentious or sentimental, and have thus failed to see that Frost's really remarkable achievement has been to maintain integrity of tone as he has. The pitch is considerably lower, the problem simpler, but the method is essentially that of the poets earlier discussed.

One of his best examples of management of tone occurs in "After Apple-Picking," a poem in which he extends his symbolism further, and achieves more intensity, than is usual for him. But to demonstrate this is to indicate that the poem is in reality a symbolist poem. [114]

The concrete experience of apple-picking is communicated firmly and realistically; but the poem invites a metaphorical

---

[3] From *Modern Poetry and The Tradition,* Chapel Hill: University of North Carolina, 1939, pp. 114-116.

extension. The task of apple-picking, it is suggested, is any task; it is life.

The drowsiness which the speaker feels after the completion of the task is associated with the cycle of the seasons. Its special character is emphasized by a bit of magic, even though the magic is whimsical:

> Essence of winter sleep is on the night,
> The scent of apples: I am drowsing off.
> I cannot rub the strangeness from my sight
> I got from looking through a pane of glass
> I skimmed this morning from the drinking trough
> And held against the world of hoary grass.
> It melted, and I let it fall and break.

The speaker goes on to speculate playfully on the form that his dreaming will take. It will surely be about apples, for his instep arch still feels the pressures of the ladder rung, and his ears are still full of the rumble of apples rolling into the cellar bin. But he returns to the subject of his drowsiness, and the phrase, "whatever sleep it is," renews the suggestion that his sleepiness may not be merely ordinary human sleepiness:

> Were he not gone,
> The woodchuck could say whether it's like his
> Long sleep, as I describe its coming on,
> Or just some human sleep.

The end of the labor leaves the speaker with a sense of completion and fulfillment—in short, with a sense of ripeness which savors of the fruit with which he has been working and of the season in which the work has been done. The ice sheet through which he has looked signals the termination of the harvest and the summons to the winter sleep of nature. The woodchuck has already begun his hibernation. The speaker does not over-emphasize his own [115] connection with nature—the reference to the woodchuck is merely one more piece of whimsy—but the connection is felt.

The poem even suggests that the sleep is like the sleep of death. We are not to feel that the speaker is necessarily conscious of this. But perhaps we are to feel that, were the analogy to present itself to him, he would accept it. In the context defined in the poem, death might be considered as something eminently

4

natural, as a sense of fulfillment mixed with a great deal of honest weariness and a sense of something well done—though with too much drowsiness for one to bother that every one of the apples had not been picked. The theme thus turns out to be a sort of rustic New England version of "Ripeness is all," though the theme is arrived at casually—stumbled over, almost—and with no effect of literary pretentiousness. [116]

Two Tramps in Mud Time

Out of the mud two strangers came
And caught me splitting wood in the yard.
And one of them put me off my aim
By hailing cheerily 'Hit them hard!'
I knew pretty well why he dropped behind
And let the other go on a way.
I knew pretty well what he had in mind:
He wanted to take my job for pay.

Good blocks of oak it was I split,
As large around as the chopping block;
And every piece I squarely hit
Fell splinterless as a cloven rock.
The blows that a life of self-control
Spares to strike for the common good
That day, giving a loose to my soul,
I spent on the unimportant wood.

The sun was warm but the wind was chill.
You know how it is with an April day
When the sun is out and the wind is still,
You're one month on in the middle of May.
But if you so much as dare to speak,
A cloud comes over the sunlit arch,
A wind comes off a frozen peak,
And you're two months back in the middle of March.

4 A bluebird comes tenderly up to alight
And turns to the wind to unruffle a plume
His song so pitched as not to excite
A single flower as yet to bloom.
It is snowing a flake: and he half knew
Winter was only playing possum.
Except in color he isn't blue,
But he wouldn't advise a thing to blossom.

5 The water for which we may have to look
In summertime with a witching-wand,
In every wheelrut's now a brook,
In every print of a hoof a pond.
Be glad of water, but don't forget
The lurking frost in the earth beneath
That will steal forth after the sun is set
And show on the water its crystal teeth.

6 The time when most I loved my task
These two must make me love it more
By coming with what they came to ask.
You'd think I never had felt before
The weight of an ax-head poised aloft,
The grip on earth of outspread feet.
The life of muscles rocking soft
And smooth and moist in vernal heat.

7 Out of the woods two hulking tramps
(From sleeping God knows where last night,
But not long since in the lumber camps).
They thought all chopping was theirs of right.
Men of the woods and lumberjacks,
They judged me by their appropriate tool.
Except as a fellow handled an ax,
They had no way of knowing a fool.

6

8 Nothing on either side was said.
They knew they had but to stay their stay
And all their logic would fill my head:
As that I had no right to play
With what was another man's work for gain.
My right might be love but theirs was need.
And where the two exist in twain
Theirs was the better right—agreed.

9 But yield who will to their separation,
My object in living is to unite
My avocation and my vocation
As my two eyes make one in sight.
Only where love and need are one,
And the work is play for mortal stakes,
Is the deed ever really done
For Heaven and the future's sakes.

❀ REGINALD L. COOK[4]

An effective illustration of the movement and temper of
Frost's mind, "Two Tramps in Mud Time" starts characteristically with the particular and ends with the general. The play of
the poet's mind as the poem unfolds indicates a considerable range
of mood from affection to irony and also a spread of awareness,
which includes awareness of self, others and the world of nature.
In structure its nine stanzas present a logical flow of reactions.
The first stanza satisfies the three unities of time, place and action.
The second stanza is concerned with self-justification. The third,
fourth and fifth stanzas amplify the vagaries of New England
seasonal climate. The sixth stanza embodies the chopper's
euphoria. The seventh stanza shifts the point of view from the
interrupted chopper to the appraising lumberjacks. The eighth
stanza points up the situation of the man who chops for love and

[4] From *The Dimensions of Robert Frost*, New York: Rinehart, 1958,
pp. 122-123.

the needy wayfarers who eye him in their extremity. The ninth stanza fuses the co-ordinates of love and need, and reconciles the tension which is psychological as well as economic. . . .

The underlying theme is a defense of the individual against the "gang security" of those who would without examining the situation suppress his effort because they think they know better how to regiment security. In effect, it is a political poem and embodies the core of [122] an important problem. When does a man's self-selected independent effort impinge on, interfere with, or violate the welfare of others? In converse the problem is, what justifies another man's appropriation of one's honorably and competently performed self-selected task? Frost reconciles the tension between heart and need when he says:

> Only where love and need are one,
> And the work is play for mortal stakes,
> Is the deed ever really done
> For Heaven and the future's sakes.

The key word here is the penultimate word "mortal" in the second line. For the poet isn't sentimental; he knows we have no right to exercise a personal indulgence willfully, arrogantly and sportively when others are in dire need or distress. When we unite our love and need in work that is play for *mortal* stakes, then the motive is pure and the act is justified. His relationship to his fellow man is one of sympathetic understanding. Moreover, it is ruggedly independent and coolly philosophical. It will take more than Steinbeck's Joads or the combined rationalization of labor leaders to outsmart this tough logic. But this is not a political poem in the usual sense. It has nothing to do with voting the Republican or Democratic ticket. It is at once more specific in its personal psychological approach to the problem of living one's life, and more general in its advocacy, like Emerson and Thoreau, of the higher, more conscientious individualism. Individualism sans conscience is amoral Nietzscheanism and leads to *Machpolitik*. Such individualism is the opposite of Frost's belief. [123]

Frost's "Two Tramps in Mud Time" is a narrative all the details of which point to the controlling and central idea of a delicately poised equilibrium: the desire, means, and necessity of attaining balance are the subject behind the incident. The amateur woodchopper and two tramps represent contrasting attitudes toward human goals and endeavor (here, in parable, the job of splitting wood). The former desires "to unite My avocation and my vocation As my two eyes make one in sight" —that is, to achieve depth and dimension; but the tramps' philosophy is single and inadequate: "Except as a fellow handled an ax, They had no way of knowing a fool." One strives toward the unity of "A Full-time Interest" (the poem's subtitle); the others would separate avocation and vocation, love and need, play and work, "mortal stakes" and "Heaven and the future's sakes." The speaker lives a life of human self-control; but the tramps, in the poem's first phrase, come "out of the mud," like sub-human creatures, and, as is implied in the parentheses in stanza 7, live without a regulated principle of self-control. Their disruptive effect is immediately evidenced, when the cheery greeting only serves to put the speaker off his "aim"—both his immediate target and his larger goal in life. The narrative proper now halts for three stanzas while the speaker characterizes "mud time," "when most I loved my task." This description is highly pertinent, consisting of a series of details illustrating April's delicate equilibrium between warmth and cold, spring and winter. The balance is extremely precarious: ". . . if you so much as dare to speak" it is disturbed. Likewise, the bluebird alights "tenderly" and sings so "as not to excite A single flower as yet to bloom." And although spring freshets flow freely, the "lurking frost" can put a glaze over the water. This season, with its union of opposites, appeals to the speaker's desire for richness and roundedness; and now, with the intrusion of the strangers, he senses another kind of balance—this one within himself. At

---

[5] "Frost's 'Two Tramps in Mud Time,' " *Explicator*, XII (June 1954), item 51.

the end, the speaker is balancing the claims of the woodchoppers against his own, but he does not tell the end of the incident. Who finished the actual chopping is unimportant; what is important is man's need to achieve personal equilibrium which is not the static dead-level of passivity but a dynamic one which arises from the resolution of opposing forces, claims, and ideals. In the very act of attempting to maintain this tricky balance are found both fulfillment and delight.

⚘ LAWRANCE THOMPSON[6]

In Frost's attitude toward life there is a very close relationship between self-discovery and the apparently trivial form-giving. The process of finding self is a circular one, as is all reasoning. We venture outward into experience and the outer experience brings us back into a new self-knowledge. He has spoken of how the writing of a poem is akin to going to the North Pole: to see if the adventurer could get back! The writer later ventures into print, not to see if he can write but to wager that he can; and when he is recognized by others, he is back to self again. Falling in love is another kind of excursion outside self to find self. But Frost's most persistent suggestions of falling in love include the love of labor because of a kind of sympathy that is developed between the actor, the act, and the thing acted upon. In all his metaphors of farm labor, reference to "the earnest love" and "the sweetest dream" is tied up to a broadening of perceptions. Horizons are pushed back. Through the action comes a sympathy not only for the rhythmical pattern of natural life but also for the shared experiences of human life. And gradually the doing is related to larger and larger significance. Out of the slight pleasure of doing comes the need for finding larger means of form-giving. And, on the other hand, out of the need for that which keeps body and soul together comes the pleasure in the doing. The two relate themselves until the hard work becomes play. Frost develops this same theme in his narrative of two tramps looking for work and finding the poet splitting his own wood: [Thompson then quotes the last two stanzas of the poem].

---

[6] From *Fire and Ice*, New York: Holt, 1942, pp. 211-212.

[211] Out of the need for doing, pleasure; out of the pleasure of doing, the deed—and from the two in one, the thing done well and with meaning. [212]

Stopping by Woods on a Snowy Evening

Whose woods these are I think I know.
His house is in the village though;
He will not see me stopping here
To watch his woods fill up with snow.

My little horse must think it queer
To stop without a farmhouse near
Between the woods and frozen lake
The darkest evening of the year.

He gives his harness bells a shake
To ask if there is some mistake.
The only other sound's the sweep
Of easy wind and downy flake.

The woods are lovely, dark and deep,
But I have promises to keep,
And miles to go before I sleep,
And miles to go before I sleep.

❦ ROBERT FROST[7]

. . . When he reads "Departmental," which he once referred to as "my iridium poem; it's hard and useful," he says, ironically, that he intends sometime to write thirty pages of notes for the

[7] Quoted by Reginald L. Cook, "Robert Frost's Asides on His Poetry," *American Literature*, XIX (January 1948), 355, 357, 358.

scholiasts. He once remarked that "Stopping by Woods on a Snowy Evening" was the kind of poem he'd like to print on one page, to be followed with "forty pages of footnotes." [355]

"Stopping by Woods on a Snowy Evening" contains "all I ever knew." [357]

. . . "Stopping by Woods on a Snowy Evening" is, he says, "a series of almost reckless commitments. I feel good in having guarded it so. [It is] . . . my heavy duty poem to be examined for the rime pairs." [358]

✻ ROBERT FROST[8]

. . . "That one I've been more bothered with than anybody has ever been with any poem in just pressing it for more than it should be pressed for. It means enough without its being pressed." And, in a biting tone, he adds, "I don't say that somebody shouldn't press it, but I don't want to be there." Often he has spoken out against the "pressers" and over-readers. "You don't want the music outraged." And of "Stopping by Woods" he says that all it means is "it's all very nice but I must be getting along, getting home." Yet no true reader leaves the discussion there. He knows as well as the poet does that what is important is how the poet played with "the constant symbol" implicit in the making of the poem. "Everything is hinting," Frost reminds us. [64]

. . . "Stopping by Woods" came to him after he had been working all night on his long poem entitled "New Hampshire." He went outside to look at the sun and it came to him. "I always thought," he explains, "it was the product of autointoxication coming from tiredness." [66]

---

[8] Quoted by Reginald L. Cook, "Frost on Frost: The Making of Poems," *American Literature*, XXVIII (March 1956), 64, 66.

✤ ROBERT FROST[9]

The most acerbic and closest-cropped expressions of his [Frost's] wit are reserved for the analysts of literature who try to pick a poem clean or miss its intent. When a friendly critic asked if the last two lines in "Stopping by Woods" referred to going to Heaven, and, by implication, death, the poet replied, "No, all that means is to get the hell out of there." [33]

. . . Frost starts out perfectly free in his poem. "I can have my first line any way I please," he says, and he is right. "But once I say a line I am committed. The first line *is* a commitment. *Whose woods these are I think I know.* Eight syllables, four beats—a line—we call it iambic. I'm not terribly [78] committed there. I can do a great many things. I did not choose the metre. What we have in English is mostly iambic anyway. When most of it is iambic, you just fall into that. *His house is in the village though*— the second line. I might be committed to couplets. If I had made another couplet beside that—a rhyme pair—I'd be in for it. I'd have to have couplets all the way. I was dancing still. I was free. Then I committed a stanza:

> Whose woods these are I think I know.
> His house is in the village though;
> He will not see me stopping here
> To watch his woods fill up with snow.

He will not see me stopping here is uncommitted. For the three rhymes in the next stanza, I picked up the unrhymed line in the first stanza and rhymed its end-rhyme 'here' with 'queer,' 'near' and 'year,' and for the third stanza I picked up 'lake' from the unrhymed line in the second stanza and rhymed it with 'shake,' 'mistake' and 'flake.' For the fourth stanza I picked up 'sweep' from the unrhymed line in the third stanza, to rhyme with 'deep' and 'sleep.'

"Every step you take is a further commitment. It is like going

---

[9] Quoted by Reginald L. Cook, *The Dimensions of Robert Frost*, New York: Rinehart, 1958, pp. 33, 78-80.

to the North Pole. If you go, you have to bring back witnesses
—some Eskimos! How was I going to get out of that stanza?
It's going to be like the Arabian Nights—one story after another.
By the third stanza you have a sense of how long a poem is going
to be. It's 'sweep' I'm commited to:

> The woods are lovely, dark and deep,
> But I have promises to keep,
> And miles to go before I sleep,
> And miles to go before I sleep.

For my poem is a commitment to convention. That's what it's a
symbol of. The form of regular verse—Greek, Latin, English—
is a symbol of commitment.

"The interest is the quarrel with those commitments. When I
read a poem, I ask myself: What is the main point in the argument? Where is the insincerity in the argument? Having committed ourselves to go to the North Pole or to our love, we have
to believe we have been to [79] the North Pole or that we have
been in love. The modern poet who uses free verse or new experiments quarrels with the commitment to convention. His revolt
is based on that, that all life goes false by its commitments. Consequently, I look at a poem very examiningly, very suspiciously.
I don't want to think that the poem is a compromise with the
rhyme." [80]

❦ LAWRANCE THOMPSON[10]

. . . In fair warning, I must confess that I do not know the
story as to how Robert Frost happened to write this poem. But
my guess, even if it should prove wrong in specific details, may
still have validity as a general illustration of that process which
I am trying to clarify. The poem is a dramatic lyric which
breaks into the middle of an incident, so that there is a drama-
in-miniature revealed with setting and lighting and actors and
properties complete. At the beginning, the reader finds the cur-
tain going up on a little action which approaches the climax
of an experience, real or imagined; that is, an experience which

---

[10] From *Fire and Ice*, New York: Holt, 1942, pp. 25-27.

14

happened to the poet or one which came to the mind of the poet as possible. A rural traveler is the actor whose brief soliloquy describes the circumstances under which he has stopped his horse-drawn sleigh to enjoy, in spite of cold and loneliness, the strange beauty of white snowflakes falling against a background of dark trees. There are many reasons why he should not stop; common-sense reasons which seem to occur even to the traveler's little horse. But the spell of the moment is so strong that the traveler is reluctant to leave, regardless of the winter night and the cold storm. He is impelled to move on by the realization of duties and distances; those "promises" which he must keep and the "miles to go" before he completes his journey. Thus the poem ends, and the images which crowd the statements are direct and unmistakable. Where, in such lines, does the emotional tension resolve itself into the mental focus of a metaphor? If this simple little [25] poem is to be considered as one in which the resolution suggests two planes of reference, the reader must be made aware of words and images which face two ways at once. Considered from the viewpoint of the poetic impulse, it is quite probable that the poet, impelled emotionally to record this real or imagined experience, did not immediately see in it any metaphorical correspondence between the sight of the moment and the insight of the past-in-the-present. Yet a correspondence appears with dramatic clarity in the final stanza. The reader is aware of more than one possible meaning for such words as "promises" and "miles" and "sleep." And it is probable that the poet also came upon these words with a conscious perception and recognition of a rational focus which grew out of this moment first felt vaguely and emotionally in the form of an inner tension. Almost with a sense of surprise the poet may have found a second plane of reference which gave deeper importance to the little incident which became the poem. But Frost's characteristic reticence and shyness, a part of his New England heritage, led him to be satisfied with those three words which suggest, without explanation or elaboration, the rationally perceived focus of this correspondence.

Each reader has no difficulty in making an elaboration from this implied metaphor. In the poem, the specific incident has completely displaced the general analogy. If a reader is satisfied to settle for the specific as satisfactory in itself, there is nothing to hinder him from so doing. On the other hand, if he wishes to continue with the extensions of the metaphor, there is nothing to hinder him from that added pleasure. The most obvious correspondence would suggest the analogy between the specific experience of the rural traveler and the general experience of any individual whose life is so frequently described as a journey; a journey including pleasures and hardships, duties and distances. In the light of such analogies, the other images offer correspondences which are valid. There is even a slightly tragic implication suggested by "the coldest evening of the year." Yet within this bitter cold occurs an elementary revelation of beauty which lays claim on us as existing nowhere else. Regardless of the dark and cold, we are prone to tarry quite irrationally because of this [26] paradoxically somber excitement and recompense. The reluctance to leave becomes an expression of the endless hunger for holding and making permanent a dark moment of pleasurable discovery in a transient experience. But we are impelled forward and away by other and inevitable commitments. There are the "promises" which we have made to ourselves and to others, or which others have made for us. And there are the "miles" we must travel through other kinds of experience before we yield to that final and inevitable commitment: sleep in death.

I am well aware that this kind of metaphorical extension is distasteful to some, and is frequently branded by others as impressionistic nonsense. I am equally sure that any poet who uses metaphors with the deliberate purpose of suggesting more than is stated offers his readers, through the very nature of his method, the freedom to read the poem on as many different planes of reference as may be discovered. The only restriction is that such induced correspondences must not be made if they invalidate the initial relationship of the specifics to each other. The rules of the game are as old as poetry. Children derive much pleasure from playing with those square boxes of different sizes which may be put together, one inside another, until they are contained within a single block. They may be treated without imagination as a single block, but the pleasure begins when they are telescoped outward. In a restricted sense, the pleasure derived from opening up a metaphor may be compared to the pleasure derived from opening up that single block which has so many proportionate identities hidden within it. [27]

❧ RENÉ WELLEK AND AUSTIN WARREN[11]

When we get beyond "private symbolism" and "traditional symbolism," there is, at the other pole, a kind of public "natural" symbolism which offers its own difficulties. Frost's poems, some of the best of them, use natural symbols the reference of which we find it difficult to control: we think of "The Road Not Taken," "Walls," "The Mountain." In "Stopping by Woods," "miles to go before I sleep" is literally true of the traveler, we assume; but in the language of natural symbolism, to "sleep" is [194] to "die"; and if one couples by contrast the "woods are lovely, dark and deep" (all three adjectives panegyric) with the moral and social check of "promises to keep," one can't wholly reject the passing, not insisted on, equation of aesthetic contemplation with some kind of ceasing to be as a responsible person. Presumably no constant reader of poetry will go wrong with Frost; but, partly because of his natural symbolism, Frost has drawn a wide audience, some of whom, once grasping the possibility of symbols, will bear down too heavily on both the natural symbols and their companions, giving to his plurisigns a fixity and rigidity alien to the nature of poetic statement, especially contemporary poetic statement. [195]

❧ LEONARD UNGER AND WILLIAM VAN O'CONNOR[12]

"Stopping by Woods on a Snowy Evening," like Milton's sonnet on his blindness and Arnold's "Dover Beach," seems to have established itself [597] permanently in anthologies and textbooks of poetry. It is one of Frost's best-known poems, and we might discover, if we had the means, that it is one of the best-known poems of the twentieth century. Its wide appeal, like that of Frost's work in general, is not difficult to explain. With the

---

[11] From *Theory of Literature*, New York: Harcourt, Brace, 1949, pp. 194-195.
[12] From *Poems for Study*, New York: Rinehart, 1953, pp. 597-600.

17

clearest and simplest language, organized in a form that is catchy and easily remembered, Frost's poem evokes a common human experience of the beauty of nature. If one has not actually had such an experience, it is at least of a kind that one can easily imagine. The quality of the experience is made available by the poem.

In other words, the poem produces an immediate and clear effect. Our description of this effect has been simple—indeed, too simple. When we dwell further on the poem and examine its several parts and aspects, we discover that there is considerably more that can be said by way of interpreting it and of explaining its effect. We should notice, for example, that the poem is not primarily the description of natural scenery but the dramatic utterance of a person on the occasion of experiencing the scene, of being *in* the scene: the utterance is in the present tense. . . . Frost's poem gives us a scene, but it seems to be giving it to us only incidentally, not by direct and calculated description. We may assume that the indirection is calculated, however natural and casual the poem may seem as a statement.

Consider first the scene and then the means by which it is portrayed. The speaker is passing deep woods on a dark night. Across the road from the woods is a frozen lake. No houses are in sight. It is snowing heavily, and a gentle, soft sound is made by the wind and by the snow falling into the woods. And now consider how the scene emerges. The poem opens with immediate reference to the woods, but they are mentioned by way of observing that their owner is a certain man who lives in the village. Since he does live in the village, we are told, he will not see the speaker looking at his property. Whether or not he will see the speaker seems a pointless concern, certainly not a very interesting or serious one, yet natural and plausible enough—the sort of thought that might pass through anyone's mind under the circumstances. This thought is uttered, and as it concludes we learn about the snow. The second and third stanzas introduce in like manner the other details of the scene. In each of these stanzas the details are parts of the fond and whimsical speculations about the little horse. It is only in the last stanza that the [598] speaker remarks directly, but briefly, upon the appearance and quality of the woods. They are "lovely, dark and deep." And in the closing lines the speaker says, or implies clearly, that he must leave the scene of the woods and be getting along. The indirect way in which the scene is described and the intermixture of casualness and whimsy are characteristic of the poetry of Frost and of the twentieth century. One can imagine a poem that might begin with the line, "The woods are lovely, dark and deep," and then proceed through a series of exclamatory appreciations to end with a general statement on nature and what it means to man, or to the poet. The climax and conclusion of such a poem would be an interpretation of what had gone before.

Frost's poem obviously contains no explicit interpretation. It may, nonetheless, be found significant beyond the scene and situation which it presents—that is, the poem is its own interpretation in that it implies some meanings in addition to those which are directly stated. We have already noticed that the poem has a particular kind of development. The scene is presented with some indirection. It is considered as someone's property and from the playfully imagined point of view of the little horse. That is, the speaker is not utterly absorbed in the scene. Although he responds to its loveliness, he is not so possessed by it that other thoughts, casual and whimsical, may not enter his mind. The implication is that the speaker does not forsake or forget all his other attitudes while he experiences the loveliness of the woods. His sensibility and appreciation exist among other attitudes and habits of mind, and they are therefore not put in the foreground of the poem.

These implications, which follow from the development of the poem, may be called immediate implications, for there are others less immediate. While the implications already mentioned qualify the speaker's act of contemplating the woods, there are implications which differentiate the several attitudes from which the woods may be regarded. From the first stanza we learn that they are the property of a man who lives in the village. The implication is that they represent an economic value and a practical purpose, as distinguished from their aspect as a lovely object to be watched, to be contemplated. In the second and third stanzas the playful remarks about the horse indicate that he is an animal that has been conditioned to a routine of purposeful behavior, and they thus imply that the speaker's behavior is not, in a sense, purposeful. He has stopped in order to watch the woods and the snow, and he watches toward no other end, but just for watching, for contemplating, for appreciating.

This implication is even clearer in the last stanza. The woods are unusually lovely, but the speaker must eventually be about his business and his responsibilities. There are still other implications in this stanza. The woods are symbolic of beauty in general, of esthetic value. This [599] symbolism is enforced by the word *"but"* in the second line. If it were not for the promises and the miles, what would the speaker do? He might watch the woods indefinitely—he might devote his life to the experience of esthetic value. Or he might enter the woods, for it is their interior, their darkness and depth, which is lovely, and which thus suggests the peacefulness of death. In their fullest symbolic potentiality, then, the woods equate death with an exclusive commitment to esthetic value. The final lines of the poem have implications which are in accord with this interpretation. The speaker feels the urge to escape into loveliness, into the peacefulness of death, but he also acknowledges the fact that there are other values and other urges. He is committed to life, in all its diversity and complexity, and he wants to go on living, to fulfill that commitment, for death will come in time—"And miles to go before I sleep." The repetition of this last line, while it successfully closes the formal pattern of the poem, also emphasizes the symbolic function of the statement.

Considerable interpretive pressure has been put upon Frost's poem, but the poem can withstand this pressure. The ultimate meanings that are found, the less immediate implications, fit nicely with those which are more immediate and obvious. For example, the life-death tension (or dilemma) which is both raised and resolved in the last stanza is logically related to earlier parts of the poem—to the tension between the speaker's contemplation of the woods and his passing thoughts about their owner and the little horse. In its ultimate implication, the last stanza summarizes and generalizes some of the meanings of the foregoing stanzas. This development is marked also by the slight shift of tone which occurs with the last stanza, for the whimsy and playfulness of the earlier stanzas do not continue in the last. [600]

ॐ JOHN CIARDI[13]

The School System has much to say these days of the virtue of reading widely, and not enough about the virtues of reading less but in depth. There are any number of reading lists for poetry, but there is not enough talk about individual poems. Poetry, finally, is one poem at a time. To read any one poem carefully is the ideal preparation for reading another. Only a poem can illustrate how poetry works.

Above, therefore, is a poem—one of the master lyrics of the English language, and almost certainly the best-known poem by an American poet. What happens in it?—which is to say, not *what* does it mean, but *how* does it mean? How does it go about being a human reenactment of a human experience? The author—perhaps the thousandth reader would need to be told —is Robert Frost.

Even the TV audience can see that this poem begins as a seemingly-simple narration of a seemingly-simple incident but ends by suggesting meanings far beyond anything specifically referred to in the narrative. And even readers with only the most casual interest in poetry might be made to note the additional fact that, though the poem suggests those larger meanings, it is very careful never to abandon its pretense to being simple narration. There is duplicity at work. The poet pretends to be talking about one thing, and all the while he is talking about many others.

Many readers are forever unable to accept the poet's essential duplicity. It is almost safe to say that a poem is never about what it seems to be about. As much could be said of the proverb. The bird in the hand, the rolling stone, the stitch in time never (except by an artful double-deception) intend any sort of statement about birds, stones, or sewing. The incident of this poem, one must conclude, is at root a metaphor.

Duplicity aside, this poem's movement from the specific to the general illustrates one of the basic formulas [13] of all poetry.

---

[13] "Robert Frost: The Way to the Poem," *Saturday Review*, XL (April 12, 1958), 13-15, 65.

Such a grand poem as Arnold's "Dover Beach" and such lesser, though unfortunately better known, poems as Longfellow's "The Village Blacksmith" and Holmes's "The Chambered Nautilus" are built on the same progression. In these three poems, however, the generalization is markedly set apart from the specific narration, and even seems additional to the telling rather than intrinsic to it. It is this sense of division one has in mind in speaking of "a tacked-on moral."

There is nothing wrong-in-itself with a tacked-on moral. Frost, in fact, makes excellent use of the device at times. In this poem, however, Frost is careful to let the whatever-the-moral-is grow out of the poem itself. When the action ends the poem ends. There is no epilogue and no explanation. Everything pretends to be about the narrated incident. And that pretense sets the basic tone of the poem's performance of itself.

The dramatic force of that performance is best observable, I believe, as a progression in three scenes.

In scene one, which coincides with stanza one, a man—a New England man—is driving his sleigh somewhere at night. It is snowing, and as the man passes a dark patch of woods he stops to watch the snow descend into the darkness. We know, moreover, that the man is familiar with these parts (he knows who owns the woods and where the owner lives), and we know that no one has seen him stop. As scene one forms itself in the theatre of the mind's-eye, therefore, it serves to establish some as yet unspecified relation between the man and the woods.

It is necessary, however, to stop here for a long parenthesis: Even so simple an opening statement raises any number of questions. It is impossible to address all the questions that rise from the poem stanza by stanza, but two that arise from stanza one illustrate the sort of thing one might well ask of the poem detail by detail.

Why, for example, does the man not say what errand he is on? What is the force of leaving the errand generalized? He might just as well have told us that he was going to the general store, or returning from it with a jug of molasses he had promised to bring Aunt Harriet and two suits of long underwear he had promised to bring the hired man. Frost, moreover, can handle homely detail to great effect. He preferred to leave his motive generalized. Why?

And why, on the other hand, does he say so much about knowing the absent owner of the woods and where he lives? Is it simply that one set of details happened-in whereas another did not? To speak of things "happening-in" is to assault the integrity of a poem. Poetry cannot be discussed meaningfully unless one can assume that everything in the poem—every last comma and variant spelling—is in it by the poet's specific act of choice. Only bad poets allow into their poems what is haphazard or cheaply chosen.

The errand, I will venture a bit brashly for lack of space, is left generalized in order the more aptly to suggest *any* errand in life and, therefore, life itself. The owner is there because he is one of the forces of the poem. Let it do to say that the force he represents is the village of mankind (that village at the edge of winter) from which the poet finds himself separated (has separated himself?) in his moment by the woods (and to which, he recalls finally, he has promises to keep). The owner is he-who-lives-in-his-village-house, thereby locked away from the poet's awareness of the-time-the-snow-tells as it engulfs and obliterates the world the village man allows himself to believe he "owns." Thus, the owner is a representative of an order of reality from which the poet has divided himself for the moment, though to a certain extent he ends by reuniting with it. Scene one, therefore, establishes not only a relation between the man and the woods, but the fact that the man's relation begins with his separation (though momentarily) from mankind.

End parenthesis one, begin parenthesis two.

Still considering the first scene as a kind of dramatic performance of forces, one must note that the poet has meticulously matched the simplicity of his language to the pretended simplicity of the narrative. Clearly, the man stopped because the beauty of the scene moved him, but he neither tells us that the scene is beautiful nor that he is moved. A bad writer, always ready to overdo, might have written: "The vastness gripped me, filling my spirit with the slow steady sinking of the snow's crystalline perfection into the glimmerless profundities of the hushed primeval wood." Frost's avoidance of such a spate illustrates two principles of good writing. The first, he has stated himself in "The Mowing": "Anything *more* than the truth would have seemed too weak" (italics mine). Understatement is one of the basic sources of power in English poetry. The second principle is to let the action speak for itself. A good novelist does not tell us that a given character is good or bad (at least not since the passing of the Dickens tradition): he shows us the character in action and then, watching him, we know. Poetry, too, has fictional obligations: even when the characters are ideas and metaphors rather than people, they must be *characterized in action*. A poem does not *talk about* ideas; it *enacts* them. The force of the poem's performance, in fact, is precisely to act out (and thereby to make us act out empathically, that is, *to feel out*, that is, *to identify with*) the speaker and why he stopped. The man is the principle actor in this little "drama of why" and in scene one he is the only character, though as noted, he is somehow related to the absent owner.

End second parenthesis.

In scene two (stanzas two and three) a *foil* is introduced. In fiction and drama, a foil is a character who "plays against" a more important character. By presenting a different point of view or an opposed set of motives, the foil moves the more important character to react in ways that might not have found expression without such opposition. The more important character is thus more fully revealed—to the reader and to himself. The foil here is the horse.

The horse forces the question. Why did the man stop? Until it occurs to him that his "little horse must think it queer" he had not asked himself for reasons. He had simply stopped. But the man finds himself faced with the question he imagines the horse to be asking: what *is* there to stop for out there in the cold, away from bin and stall (house and village and mankind?) and all that any self-respecting beast could value on such a night? In sensing that other view, the man is forced to examine his own more deeply.

In stanza two the question arises only as a feeling within the man. In stanza three, however (still scene two), the horse acts. He gives his harness bells a shake. "What's wrong?" he seems to say. "What are we waiting for?"

By now, obviously, the horse—without [14] losing its identity as horse—has also become a symbol. A symbol is something that stands for something else. Whatever that something else may be, it certainly begins as that order of life that does not understand

24

why a man stops in the wintry middle of nowhere to watch the snow come down. (Can one fail to sense by now that the dark and the snowfall symbolize a death-wish, however momentary, *i.e.*, that hunger for final rest and surrender that a man may feel, but not a beast?)

So by the end of scene two the performance has given dramatic force to three elements that work upon the man. There is his relation to the world of the owner. There is his relation to the brute world of the horse. And there is that third presence of the unownable world, the movement of the all-engulfing snow across all the orders of life, the man's, the owner's, and the horse's —with the difference that the man knows of that second dark-within-the-dark of which the horse cannot, and the owner will not, know.

The man ends scene two with all these forces working upon him simultaneously. He feels himself moved to a decision. And he feels a last call from the darkness: "the sweep/Of easy wind and downy flake." It would be so easy and so downy to go into the woods and let himself be covered over.

But scene three (stanza four) produces a fourth force. This fourth force can be given many names. It is certainly better, in fact, to give it many names than to attempt to limit it to one. It is social obligation, or personal commitment, or duty, or just the realization that a man cannot indulge a mood forever. All of these and more. But, finally, he has a simple decision to make. He may go into the woods and let the darkness and the snow swallow him from the world of beast and man. Or he must move on. And unless he is going to stop here forever, it is time to remember that he has a long way to go and that he had best be getting there. (So there is something to be said for the horse, too.)

Then and only then, his question driven more and more deeply into himself by these cross-forces, does the man venture a comment on what attracted him: "The woods are lovely, dark and deep." His mood lingers over the thought of that lovely dark-and-deep (as do the very syllables in which he phrases the thought), but the final decision is to put off the mood and move on. He has his man's way to go and his man's obligations to tend to before he can yield. He has miles to go before his sleep. He repeats that thought and the performance ends.

But why the repetition? The first time Frost says "And miles to go before I sleep," there can be little doubt that the primary meaning is: "I have a long way to go before I get to bed tonight." The second time he says it, however, "miles to go" and "sleep" are suddenly transformed into symbols. What are those "something-elses" the symbols stand for? Hundreds of people have tried to ask Mr. Frost that question and he has always turned it away. He has turned it away *because he cannot answer it*. He could answer some part of it. But some part is not enough.

For a symbol is like a rock dropped into a pool: it sends out ripples in all directions, and the ripples are in motion. Who can say where the last ripple disappears? One may have a sense that he knows the approximate center point of the ripples, the point at which the stone struck the water. Yet even then he has trouble marking it surely. How does one make a mark on water? Oh very well—the center point of that second "miles to go" is probably approximately in the neighborhood of being close to meaning, perhaps, "the road of life"; and the second "before I sleep" is maybe that close to meaning "before I take my final rest," the rest in darkness that seemed so temptingly dark-and-deep for the moment of the mood. But the ripples continue to move and the light to change on the water, and the longer one watches the more changes he sees. Such shifting-and-being-at-the-same-instant is of the very sparkle and life of poetry. One experiences it as one experiences life, for everytime he looks at an experience he sees something new, and he sees it change as he watches it. And that sense of continuity in fluidity is one of the primary kinds of knowledge, one of man's basic ways of knowing, and one that only the arts can teach, poetry foremost among them.

Frost himself certainly did not ask what that repeated last line meant. It came to him and he received it. He "felt right" about it. And what he "felt right" about was in no sense a "meaning" that, say, an essay could apprehend, but an act of experience that could be fully presented only by the dramatic enactment of forces which is the performance of the poem.

Now look at the poem in another way. Did Frost know what he was going to do when he began? Considering the poem simply as an act of skill, as a piece of juggling, one cannot fail to respond to the magnificent turn at the end where, with one flip, seven of the simplest words in the language suddenly dazzle full of never-ending waves of thought and feeling. Or, more precisely, of felt-thought. Certainly an equivalent stunt by a juggler—could there be an equivalent—would bring the house down. Was it to cap his performance with that grand stunt that Frost wrote the poem?

Far from it. The obvious fact is that *Frost could not have known he was going to write those lines until he wrote them.* Then a second fact must be registered: *he wrote them because, for the fun of it, he had got himself into trouble.*

Frost, like every good poet, began by playing a game with himself. The most usual way of writing a four line stanza with four feet to the line is to rhyme the third line with the first, and the fourth line with the second. Even that much rhyme is so difficult in English that many poets and almost all of the anonymous ballad makers do not bother to rhyme the first and third lines at all, settling for two rhymes in four lines as good enough. For English is a rhyme-poor language. In Italian and in French, for example, so many words end with the same sounds that rhyming is relatively easy—so easy that many modern French and Italian poets do not bother to rhyme at all. English, being a more agglomerate language, has far more final sounds, hence fewer of them rhyme. When an Italian poet writes a line ending with "vita" (life) he has literally hundreds of rhyme choices available. When an English poet writes "life" at the end of a line he can summon "strife, wife, knife, fife, rife," and then he is in trouble. Now "life-strife" and "life-rife" and "life-wife" seem to offer a combination of possible ideas that can be related by more than just the rhyme. Inevitably, therefore, the poets have had to work and rework these combinations until the sparkle has gone out of them. The reader is normally tired of such rhyme-led asso-[15]ciations. When he encounters "life-strife" he is certainly entitled to suspect that the poet did not really want to say "strife"—that had there been in English such a word as, say, "hife," meaning "infinite peace and harmony," the poet would as gladly have used that word instead of "strife." Thus, the reader feels that the writing is haphazard, that the rhyme is making the poet say things he does not really feel, and which, therefore, the reader does not feel except as boredom. One likes to see the rhymes fall into place, but he must end with the belief that it is the poet who is deciding what is said and not the rhyme scheme that is forcing the saying.

So rhyme is a kind of game, and an especially difficult one in English. As in every game, the fun of the rhyme is to set one's difficulties high and then to meet them skilfully. As Frost himself once defined freedom, it consists of "moving easy in harness."

In "Stopping by Woods on a Snowy Evening" Frost took a long chance. He decided to rhyme not two lines in each stanza, but three. Not even Frost could have sustained that much rhyme in a long poem (as Dante, for example, with the advantage of writing in Italian, sustained triple rhyme for thousands of lines in "The Divine Comedy"). Frost would have known instantly, therefore, when he took the original chance, that he was going to write a short poem. He would have had that much foretaste of it.

So the first stanza emerged rhymed a-a-b-a. And with the sure sense that this was to be a short poem, Frost decided to take an additional chance and to redouble: in English three rhymes in four lines is more than enough; there is no need to rhyme the fourth line. For the fun of it, however, Frost set himself to pick up that loose rhyme and to weave it into the pattern, thereby accepting the all but impossible burden of quadruple rhyme.

The miracle is that it worked. Despite the enormous freight of rhyme, the poem not only came out as a neat pattern, but managed to do so with no sense of strain. Every word and every rhyme falls into place as naturally and as inevitably as if there were no rhyme restricting the poet's choices.

That ease-in-difficulty is certainly inseparable from the success of the poem's performance. One watches the skill-man juggle three balls, then four, then five, and every addition makes the trick more wonderful. But unless he makes the hard trick seem as easy as an easy trick, then all is lost.

The real point, however, is not only that Frost took on a hard rhyme-trick and made it seem easy. It is rather as if the juggler, carried away, had tossed up one more ball than he could really handle, and then amazed himself by actually handling it. So with the real triumph of this poem, Frost could not have known what a stunning effect his repetition of the last line was going to produce. He could not even know he was going to repeat

28

the line. He simply found himself up against a difficulty he almost certainly had not foreseen and he had to improvise to meet it. For in picking up the rhyme from the third line of stanza one and carrying it over into stanza two, he had created an endless chain-link form within which each stanza left a hook sticking out for the next stanza to hang on. So by stanza four, feeling the poem rounding to its end, Frost had to do something about that extra rhyme.

He might have tucked it back into a third line rhyming with the *know-though-snow* of stanza one. He could thus have rounded the poem out to the mathematical symmetry of using each rhyme four times. But though such a device might be defensible in theory, a rhyme repeated after eleven lines is so far from its original rhyme sound that its feeling as rhyme must certainly be lost. And what good is theory if the reader is not moved by the writing?

It must have been in some such quandary that the final repetition suggested itself—a suggestion born of the very difficulties the poet had let himself in for. So there is that point beyond mere ease in handling a hard thing, the point at which the very difficulty offers the poet the opportunity to do better than he knew he could. What, aside from having that happen to oneself, could be more self-delighting than to participate in its happening by one's reader-identification with the poem?

And by now a further point will have suggested itself: that the human-insight of the poem and the technicalities of its poetic artifice are inseparable. Each feeds the other. That interplay is the poem's meaning, a matter not of WHAT DOES IT MEAN, for no one can ever say entirely what a good poem means, but of HOW DOES IT MEAN, a process one can come much closer to discussing.

There is a necessary epilogue. Mr. Frost has often discussed this poem on the platform, or more usually in the course of a long-evening-after a talk. Time and again I have heard him say that he just wrote it off, that it just came to him, and that he set it down as it came.

Once at Bread Loaf, however, I heard him add one very essential piece to the discussion of how it "just came." One night, he said, he had sat down after supper to work at a long piece of blank verse. The piece never worked out, but Mr. Frost found himself so absorbed in it that, when next he looked up, dawn was at his window. He rose, crossed to the window, stood looking out for a few minutes, and *then* it was that "Stopping by Woods" suddenly "just came," so that all he had to do was cross the room and write it down.

Robert Frost is the sort of artist who hides his traces. I know of no Frost worksheets anywhere. If someone has raided his wastebasket in secret, it is possible that such worksheets exist somewhere, but Frost would not willingly allow anything but the finished product to leave him. Almost certainly, therefore, no one will ever know what was in that piece of unsuccessful blank verse he had been working at with such concentration, but I for one would stake my life that could that worksheet be uncovered, it would be found to contain the germinal stuff of "Stopping by Woods"; that what was a-simmer in him all night without finding its proper form, suddenly, when he let his still-occupied mind look away, came at him from a different direction, offered itself in a different form, and that finding that form exactly right the impulse proceeded to marry itself to the new shape in one of the most miraculous performances of English lyricism.

And that, too—whether or not one can accept so hypothetical a discussion—is part of HOW the poem means. It means that marriage to the perfect form, the poem's shapen declaration of itself, its moment's monument fixed beyond all possibility of change. And thus, finally, in every truly good poem, "How does it mean?" must always be answered "Triumphantly." Whatever the poem "is about," *how* it means is always how Genesis means: the word become a form, and the form become a thing, and—when the becoming is true—the thing become a part of the knowledge and experience of the race forever. [65]

✿ ADDITIONAL
✿ POEMS

᯾᯾᯾᯾᯾᯾᯾᯾᯾᯾᯾᯾᯾᯾᯾

The Pasture

I'm going out to clean the pasture spring;
I'll only stop to rake the leaves away
(And wait to watch the water clear, I may):
I sha'n't be gone long.—You come too.

I'm going out to fetch the little calf
That's standing by the mother. It's so young
It totters when she licks it with her tongue.
I sha'n't be gone long.—You come too.

Home Burial

He saw her from the bottom of the stairs
Before she saw him. She was starting down,
Looking back over her shoulder at some fear.
She took a doubtful step and then undid it
To raise herself and look again. He spoke
Advancing toward her: 'What is it you see
From up there always—for I want to know.'
She turned and sank upon her skirts at that,
And her face changed from terrified to dull.
He said to gain time: 'What is it you see,'
Mounting until she cowered under him.
'I will find out now—you must tell me, dear.'
She, in her place, refused him any help
With the least stiffening of her neck and silence.

She let him look, sure that he wouldn't see,
Blind creature; and awhile he didn't see.
But at last he murmured, 'Oh,' and again, 'Oh.'

'What is it—what?' she said.

                           'Just that I see.'

'You don't,' she challenged. 'Tell me what it is.'

'The wonder is I didn't see at once.
I never noticed it from here before.
I must be wonted to it—that's the reason.
The little graveyard where my people are!
So small the window frames the whole of it.
Not so much larger than a bedroom, is it?
There are three stones of slate and one of marble,
Broad-shouldered little slabs there in the sunlight
On the sidehill. We haven't to mind *those*.
But I understand: it is not the stones,
But the child's mound—'

                  'Don't, don't, don't, don't,' she cried.

She withdrew shrinking from beneath his arm
That rested on the bannister, and slid downstairs;
And turned on him with such a daunting look,
He said twice over before he knew himself:
'Can't a man speak of his own child he's lost?'

'Not you! Oh, where's my hat? Oh, I don't need it!
I must get out of here. I must get air.
I don't know rightly whether any man can.'

'Amy! Don't go to someone else this time.
Listen to me. I won't come down the stairs.'

He sat and fixed his chin between his fists.
'There's something I should like to ask you, dear.'

'You don't know how to ask it.'

                        'Help me, then.'

Her fingers moved the latch for all reply.

'My words are nearly always an offense.
I don't know how to speak of anything
So as to please you. But I might be taught
I should suppose. I can't say I see how.
A man must partly give up being a man
With women-folk. We could have some arrangement
By which I'd bind myself to keep hands off
Anything special you're a-mind to name.
Though I don't like such things 'twixt those that love.
Two that don't love can't live together without them.
But two that do can't live together with them.'
She moved the latch a little. 'Don't—don't go.
Don't carry it to someone else this time.
Tell me about it if it's something human.
Let me into your grief. I'm not so much
Unlike other folks as your standing there
Apart would make me out. Give me my chance.
I do think, though, you overdo it a little.
What was it brought you up to think it the thing
To take your mother-loss of a first child
So inconsolably—in the face of love.
You'd think his memory might be satisfied—'

'There you go sneering now!'

                          'I'm not, I'm not!
You make me angry. I'll come down to you.
God, what a woman! And it's come to this,
A man can't speak of his own child that's dead.'

'You can't because you don't know how to speak.
If you had any feelings, you that dug
With your own hand—how could you?—his little grave;
I saw you from that very window there,
Making the gravel leap and leap in air,
Leap up, like that, like that, and land so lightly
And roll back down the mound beside the hole.
I thought, Who is that man? I didn't know you.
And I crept down the stairs and up the stairs
To look again, and still your spade kept lifting.
Then you came in. I heard your rumbling voice
Out in the kitchen, and I don't know why,
But I went near to see with my own eyes.
You could sit there with the stains on your shoes
Of the fresh earth from your own baby's grave
And talk about your everyday concerns.
You had stood the spade up against the wall
Outside there in the entry, for I saw it.'

'I shall laugh the worst laugh I ever laughed.
I'm cursed. God, if I don't believe I'm cursed.'

'I can repeat the very words you were saying.
"Three foggy mornings and one rainy day
Will rot the best birch fence a man can build."
Think of it, talk like that at such a time!
What had how long it takes a birch to rot
To do with what was in the darkened parlor.
You *couldn't* care! The nearest friends can go
With anyone to death, comes so far short
They might as well not try to go at all.
No, from the time when one is sick to death,
One is alone, and he dies more alone.
Friends make pretense of following to the grave,
But before one is in it, their minds are turned
And making the best of their way back to life
And living people, and things they understand.

But the world's evil. I won't have grief so
If I can change it. Oh, I won't, I won't!'

'There, you have said it all and you feel better.
You won't go now. You're crying. Close the door.
The heart's gone out of it: why keep it up.
Amy! There's someone coming down the road!'

'*You*—oh, you think the talk is all. I must go—
Somewhere out of this house. How can I make you—'

'If—you—do!' She was opening the door wider.
'Where do you mean to go? First tell me that.
I'll follow and bring you back by force. I *will!*—'

An Empty Threat

I stay;
But it isn't as if
There wasn't always Hudson's Bay
And the fur trade,
A small skiff
And a paddle blade.

I can just see my tent pegged,
And me on the floor,
Crosslegged,
And a trapper looking in at the door
With furs to sell.

His name's Joe,
Alias John,
And between what he doesn't know
And won't tell

About where Henry Hudson's gone,
I can't say he's much help;
But we get on.

The seal yelp
On an ice cake.
It's not men by some mistake?

No,
There's not a soul
For a wind-break
Between me and the North Pole—

Except always John-Joe,
My French Indian Esquimaux,
And he's off setting traps,
In one himself perhaps.

Give a head shake
Over so much bay
Thrown away
In snow and mist
That doesn't exist,
I was going to say,
For God, man or beast's sake,
Yet does perhaps for all three.

Don't ask Joe
What it is to him.
It's sometimes dim
What it is to me,
Unless it be
It's the old captain's dark fate
Who failed to find or force a strait
In its two-thousand-mile coast;
And his crew left him where he failed,
And nothing came of all he sailed.

It's to say, 'You and I'
To such a ghost,
'You and I
Off here
With the dead race of the Great Auk!'
And, 'Better defeat almost,
If seen clear,
Than life's victories of doubt
That need endless talk talk
To make them out.'

Fire and Ice

Some say the world will end in fire,
Some say in ice.
From what I've tasted of desire
I hold with those who favor fire.
But if it had to perish twice,
I think I know enough of hate
To say that for destruction ice
Is also great
And would suffice.

Dust of Snow

The way a crow
Shook down on me
The dust of snow
From a hemlock tree

Has given my heart
A change of mood
And saved some part
Of a day I had rued.

To Earthward

Love at the lips was touch
As sweet as I could bear;
And once that seemed too much;
I lived on air

That crossed me from sweet things
The flow of—was it musk
From hidden grapevine springs
Down hill at dusk?

I had the swirl and ache
From sprays of honeysuckle
That when they're gathered shake
Dew on the knuckle.

I craved strong sweets, but those
Seemed strong when I was young;
The petal of the rose
It was that stung.

Now no joy but lacks salt
That is not dashed with pain
And weariness and fault;
I crave the stain

Of tears, the aftermark
Of almost too much love,
The sweet of bitter bark
And burning clove.

When stiff and sore and scarred
I take away my hand

From leaning on it hard
In grass and sand,

The hurt is not enough:
I long for weight and strength
To feel the earth as rough
To all my length.

A Soldier

He is that fallen lance that lies as hurled,
That lies unlifted now, come dew, come rust,
But still lies pointed as it plowed the dust.
If we who sight along it round the world,
See nothing worthy to have been its mark,
It is because like men we look too near,
Forgetting that as fitted to the sphere,
Our missiles always make too short an arc.
They fall, they rip the grass, they intersect
The curve of earth, and striking, break their own;
They make us cringe for metal-point on stone.
But this we know, the obstacle that checked
And tripped the body, shot the spirit on
Further than target ever showed or shone.

A Drumlin Woodchuck

One thing has a shelving bank,
Another a rotting plank,
To give it cozier skies
And make up for its lack of size.

My own strategic retreat
Is where two rocks almost meet,

And still more secure and snug,
A two-door burrow I dug.

With those in mind at my back
I can sit forth exposed to attack
As one who shrewdly pretends
That he and the world are friends.

All we who prefer to live
Have a little whistle we give,
And flash, at the least alarm
We dive down under the farm.

We allow some time for guile
And don't come out for a while
Either to eat or drink.
We take occasion to think.

And if after the hunt goes past
And the double-barreled blast
(Like war and pestilence
And the loss of common sense),

If I can with confidence say
That still for another day,
Or even another year,
I will be there for you, my dear,

It will be because, though small
As measured against the All,
I have been so instinctively thorough
About my crevice and burrow.

Neither Out Far Nor In Deep

The people along the sand
All turn and look one way.
They turn their back on the land.
They look at the sea all day.

As long as it takes to pass
A ship keeps raising its hull;
The wetter ground like glass
Reflects a standing gull.

The land may vary more;
But wherever the truth may be—
The water comes ashore,
And the people look at the sea.

They cannot look out far.
They cannot look in deep.
But when was that ever a bar
To any watch they keep?

Come In

As I came to the edge of the woods,
Thrush music—hark!
Now if it was dusk outside,
Inside it was dark.

Too dark in the woods for a bird
By sleight of wing
To better its perch for the night,
Though it still could sing.

The last of the light of the sun
That had died in the west
Still lived for one song more
In a thrush's breast.

Far in the pillared dark
Thrush music went—
Almost like a call to come in
To the dark and lament.

But no, I was out for stars:
I would not come in.
I meant not even if asked,
And I hadn't been.

The Subverted Flower

She drew back; he was calm:
'It is this that had the power.'
And he lashed his open palm
With the tender-headed flower.
He smiled for her to smile,
But she was either blind
Or willfully unkind.
He eyed her for a while
For a woman and a puzzle.
He flicked and flung the flower,
And another sort of smile
Caught up like finger tips
The corners of his lips
And cracked his ragged muzzle.
She was standing to the waist
In goldenrod and brake,
Her shining hair displaced.
He stretched her either arm
As if she made it ache
To clasp her—not to harm;

As if he could not spare
To touch her neck and hair.
'If this has come to us
And not to me alone—'
So she thought she heard him say;
Though with every word he spoke
His lips were sucked and blown
And the effort made him choke
Like a tiger at a bone.
She had to lean away.
She dared not stir a foot,
Lest movement should provoke
The demon of pursuit
That slumbers in a brute.
It was then her mother's call
From inside the garden wall
Made her steal a look of fear
To see if he could hear
And would pounce to end it all
Before her mother came.
She looked and saw the shame:
A hand hung like a paw,
An arm worked like a saw
As if to be persuasive,
An ingratiating laugh
That cut the snout in half,
An eye become evasive.
A girl could only see
That a flower had marred a man,
But what she could not see
Was that the flower might be
Other than base and fetid:
That the flower had done but part,
And what the flower began
Her own too meager heart
Had terribly completed.
She looked and saw the worst.
And the dog or what it was,
Obeying bestial laws,
A coward save at night,

Turned from the place and ran.
She heard him stumble first
And use his hands in flight.
She heard him bark outright.
And oh, for one so young
The bitter words she spit
Like some tenacious bit
That will not leave the tongue.
She plucked her lips for it,
And still the horror clung.
Her mother wiped the foam
From her chin, picked up her comb
And drew her backward home.

❧ REVIEWS

❧ UNSIGNED REVIEW OF *A Boy's Will*[1]

We wish we could fitly express the difference which marks off *A Boy's Will* from all the other books here noticed. Perhaps it is best hinted by stating that the poems combine, with a rare sufficiency, the essential qualities of inevitability and surprise. We have read every line with that amazement and delight which are too seldom evoked by books of modern verse. Without need of qualification or a trimming of epithets, it is undoubtedly the work of a true poet. We do not need to be told that the poet is a young man: the dew and the ecstasy—the audacity, too—of pristine vision are here. At the same time, it is extraordinarily free from a young poet's extravagances; there is no insistent obtrusion of self-consciousness, no laboured painting of lilies, nothing of the plunge and strain after super-things. Neither does it belong to any modern "school," nor go in harness to any new and twisted theory of art. It is so simple, [359] lucid, and experimental that, reading a poem, one can see clearly with the poet's own swift eyes, and follow the trail of his glancing thought. One feels that this man has *seen* and *felt:* seen with a revelatory, a creative vision; felt personally and intensely; and he simply writes down, without confusion or affectation, the results thereof. Rarely today is it our fortune to fall in with a new poet expressing himself in so pure a vein. No one who really cares for poetry should miss this little book. There is scarcely a poem of them all but will reward with a thrill, and many of them will yield much more. If we must select, "The Trial by Existence" must be mentioned for power of imagination; "Pan With Us" for spirit and sufficiency and for its beautifully clean finish; "October" for its neat, skilful handling; and "Storm Fear" for its stark articulation in

---

[1] From "The Procession of the Muse," *Academy and Literature,* LXXXV (September 20, 1913) 359-360.

which every word tells. This last is well worthy of full quotation:

> When the wind works against us in the dark,
> And pelts with snow
> The lower chamber window on the east,
> And whispers with a sort of stifled bark,
> The beast,
> "Come out! Come out!"—
> It costs no inward struggle not to go,
> Ah, no!
> I count our strength,
> Two and a child,
> Those of us not asleep subdued to mark
> How the cold creeps as the fire dies at length,—
> How drifts are piled,
> Dooryard and road ungraded,
> Till even the comforting barn grows far away,
> And my heart owns a doubt
> Whether 'tis in us to arise with day
> And save ourselves unaided.

We have not the slightest idea who Mr. Robert Frost may be, but we welcome him unhesitatingly to the ranks of the poets born, and are convinced that if this is a true sample of his parts he should presently give us work far worthier of honour than much which passes for front-rank poetry at the present time. [360]

❧ EZRA POUND ON *North of Boston*[2]

It is a sinister thing that so American, I might even say so parochial, a talent as that of Robert Frost should have to be exported before it can find due encouragement and recognition.

Even Emerson had sufficient elasticity of mind to find something in the "yawp." One doesn't need to like a book or a poem or a picture in order to recognize artistic vigor. But the typical American editor of the last twenty years has resolutely shut his mind against serious American writing. I do not exaggerate, I

[2] "Modern Georgics," *Poetry*, V (December 1914), 127-130; also *The Literary Essays of Ezra Pound*, New York: New Directions, 1954, pp. 384-386. All rights reserved. Reprinted by permission of New Directions.

quote exactly, when I say that these gentlemen deliberately write to authors that such and such a matter is "too unfamiliar to our readers."

There was once an American editor who would even print me, so I showed him Frost's "Death of the Hired Man." He wouldn't have it; he had printed a weak pseudo-Masefieldian poem about a hired man two months before, one written in a stilted pseudo-literary language, with all sorts of floridities and worn-out ornaments.

Mr. Frost is an honest writer, writing from himself, from his own knowledge and emotion; not simply picking up the manner which magazines are accepting at the moment, and applying it to topics in vogue. He is quite consciously and definitely putting New England rural life into verse. He is not using themes that anybody could have cribbed out of Ovid. [127]

There are only two passions in art; there are only love and hate—with endless modifications. Frost has been honestly fond of the New England people, I dare say with spells of irritation. He has given their life honestly and seriously. He has never turned aside to make fun of it. He has taken their tragedy as tragedy, their stubbornness as stubbornness. I know more of farm life than I did before I had read his poems. That means I know more of "Life."

Mr. Frost has dared to write, and for the most part with success, in the natural speech of New England; in natural spoken speech, which is very different from the "natural" speech of the newspapers, and of many professors. His poetry is a bit slow, but you aren't held up every five minutes by the feeling that you are listening to a fool; so perhaps you read it just as easily and quickly as you might read the verse of some of the sillier and more "vivacious" writers. . . . [128]

Professors to the contrary notwithstanding, no one expects Jane Austen to be as interesting as Stendhal. A book about a dull, stupid, hemmed-in sort of life, by a person who has lived it, will never be as interesting as the work of some author who has comprehended many men's manners and seen many grades and conditions of existence. But Mr. Frost's people are distinctly real. Their speech is real; he has known them. I don't want much to meet them, but I know that they exist, and what is more, that they exist as he has portrayed them. [129]

Mr. Frost has humor, but he is not its victim. "The Code" has a pervasive humor, the humor of things as they are, not that of an author trying to be funny, or trying to "bring out" the ludicrous phase of some incident or character because he dares not rely on sheer presentation. There is nothing more nauseating to the developed mind than that sort of local buffoonery which the advertisements call "racy"—the village wit presenting some village joke which is worn out everywhere else. It is a great comfort to find someone who tries to give life, the life of the rural district, as a whole, evenly, and not merely as a hook to hang jokes on. The easiest thing to see about a man is an eccentric or worn-out garment, and one is godforsakenly tired of the post-Bret-Hartian, post-Mark-Twainian humorist.

Mr. Frost's work is not "accomplished," but it is the work of a man who will make neither concessions nor pretences. He will perform no money-tricks. His stuff sticks in your head—not his words, nor his phrases, nor his cadences, but his subject matter. You do not confuse one of his poems with another in your memory. His book is a contribution to American literature, the sort of sound work that will develop into very interesting literature if persevered in.

I don't know that one is called upon to judge between the poems in *North of Boston*. "The Death of the Hired Man" is perhaps the best, or "The Housekeeper," though here the construction is a bit straggly. There are moments in "Mending Wall." "The Black Cottage" is very clearly stated. [130]

🙚 AMY LOWELL ON *North of Boston*[3]

Some six months ago there appeared in London a modest little green-covered book, entitled *North of Boston*. It was by an American living in England, so its publication on the other side of the Atlantic came about quite naturally, and was no reflection on the perspicacity of our publishers at home. To those of us who admire Mr. Frost's book it is no small pleasure to take up this new edition, bearing an American imprint, and feel that

[3] *"North of Boston,"* New Republic, II (February 20, 1915), 81-82.

the stigma of non-comprehension so often put upon us by expatriated Americans can never be justified in this case.

Indeed, Mr. Frost is only expatriated in a physical sense. Living in England he is, nevertheless, saturated with New England. For not only is his work New England in subject, it is so in technique. No hint of European forms has crept into it. It is certainly the most American volume of poetry which has appeared for some time. I use the word American in the way it is constantly employed by contemporary reviewers, to mean work of a color so local as to be almost photographic. Mr. Frost's book is American in the sense that Whittier is American, and not at all in that subtler sense in which Poe ranks as the greatest American poet.

The thing which makes Mr. Frost's work remarkable is the fact that he has chosen to write it as verse. We have been flooded for twenty years with New England stories in prose. The finest and most discerning are the little masterpieces of Alice Brown. She too is a poet in her descriptions, she too has caught the desolation and "dourness" of lonely New England farms, but unlike Mr. Frost she has a rare sense of humor, and that, too, is of New England, although no hint of it appears in *North of Boston*. And just because of the lack of it, just because its place is taken by an irony, sardonic and grim, Mr. Frost's book reveals a disease which is eating into the vitals of our New England life, at least in its rural communities.

What is there in the hard, vigorous climate of these states which plants the seeds of degeneration? Is the violence and ugliness of their religious belief the cause of these twisted and tortured lives? Have the sane, full-blooded men all been drafted away to the cities, or the West, leaving behind only feeble remainders of a once fine stock? The question again demands an answer after the reading of Mr. Frost's book.

Other countries can rear a sturdy peasantry on the soil, a peasantry which maintains itself for generations, heavy and slow perhaps, but strong and self-replenishing; and this for a length of time beside which our New England civilization is as nothing. We are often told that the telephone has done much to decrease insanity in the farming districts, and doubtless it is true. New England winters are long and isolating. But what about Russian winters, Polish, Swedish, Norwegian? After all, the telephone is a very modern invention, and these countries have been rearing a sturdy peasantry for hundreds of years. It is said that the country people of these nations are less highly organized, less well educated, than are New Englanders, and so better able to stand the loneliness of long winters. But this does not explain the great numbers of people, sprung from old New England stock, but not themselves living in remote country places, who go insane.

It is a question for the psychiatrist to answer, and it would be interesting to ask it with *North of Boston* as a text-book to go by. Mr. Frost has reproduced both people and scenery with a vividness which is extraordinary. Here are the huge hills, undraped by any sympathetic legend, felt as things hard and unyielding, almost sinister, not exactly feared, but regarded as in some sort influences nevertheless. Here are great stretches of blueberry pasture lying in the sun; and again, autumn orchards cracking with fruit which it is almost too much trouble to gather. Heavy thunderstorms drench the lonely roads and spatter on the walls of farm-houses rotting in abandonment; and the modern New England town, with narrow frame houses, visited by drummers alone, is painted in all its ugliness. For Mr. Frost's is not the kindly New England of Whittier, nor the humorous and sensible one of Lowell; it is a latter-day New England, where a civilization is decaying to give place to another and very different one.

Mr. Frost does not deal with the changed population, with the Canadians and Finns who are taking up the deserted farms. His people are left-overs of the old stock, morbid, pursued by phantoms, slowly sinking to insanity. In "The Black Cottage" we have the pathos of the abandoned house, after the death of the stern, narrow woman who had lived in it. In "A Servant to Servants" we have a woman already insane once and drifting there again, with the consciousness that her drab, monotonous life is bringing it upon her. "Home Burial" gives the morbidness of death in these remote places; a woman unable to take up her life again when her only child had died. The charming idyll, "After Apple-Picking," is dusted over with something uncanny, and "The Fear" is a horrible revelation of those undercurrents which go on as much in the country as in the city, and with remorse eating away whatever satisfaction the following of desire might have brought. That is also the theme of "The House-keeper," while "The Generations of Men" shows that foolish pride in a useless race which is so strange a characteristic of these people. It is all here—the book is the epitome of a decaying New England. . . . [81]

I have said that Mr. Frost's work is almost photographic. The qualification was unnecessary, it is photographic. The pictures, the characters, are reproduced directly from life, they are burnt into his mind as though it were a sensitive plate. He gives out what has been put in, unchanged by any personal mental process. His imagination is bounded by what he has seen, he is confined within the limits of his experience (or at least what might have been his experience) and bent all one way like the wind-blown trees of New England hillsides.

In America we are always a little late in following artistic leads. "Les Soirées de Médun," and all Zola's long influence, are passing away in Europe. In England, even such a would-be realist as Masefield lights his stories with bursts of a very rare imagination. No such bursts flame over Mr. Frost's work. He tells you what he has seen *exactly* as he has seen it. And in the word *exactly* lies the half of his talent. The other half is a great and beautiful simplicity of phrase, the inheritance of a race brought up on the English Bible. Mr. Frost's work is not in the least objective. He is not writing of people whom he has met in summer vacations, who strike him as interesting, and whose life he thinks worthy of perpetuation. Mr. Frost writes as a man under the spell of a fixed idea. He is as racial as his own puppets. One of the great interests of the book is the uncompromising New Englander it reveals. That he could have written half so valuable a book had such not been the case I very much doubt. Art is rooted in the soil, and only the very greatest men can be both cosmopolitan and great. Mr. Frost is as New England as Burns is Scotch, Synge Irish, or Mistral Provençal.

And Mr. Frost has chosen his medium with an unerring sense of fitness. As there is no rare and vivid imaginative force playing over his subjects, so there is no exotic music pulsing through his verse. He has not been seduced into subtleties of expression which would be painfully out of place. His words are simple, straightforward, direct, manly, and there is an elemental quality in all he does which would surely be lost if he chose to pursue niceties of phrase. He writes in classic metres in a way to set the teeth of all the poets of the older schools on edge; and he writes in classic metres, and uses inversions and clichés whenever he pleases, those devices so abhorred by the newest generation. He goes his own way, regardless of anyone else's rules, and the result is a book of unusual power and sincerity. . . . [82]

❧ DAVID MORTON ON *New Hampshire*[4]

To reveal the eccentricities of temperament in a strongly charactered people, and to do this in a vivid and rememberable way, is a valuable service to the picturesque and entertaining in art. That it is not the very greatest achievement possible to poetry needs but to be stated to be self-evident. Beyond that lies the revelation of the profound and essential and universal qualities of the human spirit that underlie all peculiarities of temperament, all accident of environment. Mr. Frost, we are led to believe, would be the first to disclaim any attempt at this latter and ampler task, and declare his purposes in terms of the former. In fact, in the title poem in this collection he says, perhaps with not quite this meaning, but certainly with exact identification: "I'm what is called . . . an environmentalist."

To the consistent reader of Frost *New Hampshire* will represent a definite—if not final—choice of direction among several tendencies discernible in the earlier books. One may, for reasons of taste and others, quarrel with that choice. But the success of the achievement in the chosen field is beyond cavil. What he has elected to do he has done vividly and with telling and haunting effect. And that is to present in heightened and intense light and shadow the peculiar character of a people in a special environment. Thus the whole aim is special and peculiar and restricted. It is not the universal human qualities underlying all temperamental divergencies which interest him, but these divergencies themselves.

This is the theme of Mr. Frost's latest volume as a whole. It is the part of his work, moreover, which has attracted most attention and which in the mind of the public has defined his place.

---

[4] "The Poet of the New Hampshire Hills," *Outlook*, CXXXV (December 19, 1923), 688-689.

One hears little enough of some of the earlier poems—and indeed some of the later—which partake of this character not at all. One is led to believe that in this Mr. Frost's aim and the public's definition are at one; for in all his writing after *A Boy's Will* there is a perceptible progression in this department of his work. It is a far cry, for example, from "A Prayer in Spring," typical of the poetry in *A Boy's Will*, to—let us say—"The Axe-Helve," in the latest volume. Yet it is the same poet writing; one feels the same personality behind the two, the same distinctive quality of mind. And the connecting links are to be found in the books *North of Boston* and *Mountain Interval.* One reads *A Boy's Will* and sees several possible lines of development, and in *Mountain Interval* and *North of Boston* encounters less of pure lyricism or universal emotions and more attention to the eccentricities of a peculiar people dominated and shaped by a peculiar environment, and thus is prepared for *New Hampshire,* so large a part of which is given over to this undertaking. Read, for example, this "Prayer in Spring," from *A Boy's Will:*

"A Prayer in Spring"

Oh, give us pleasure in the flowers today;
And give us not to think so far away
As the uncertain harvest; keep us here
All simply in the springing of the year.

Oh, give us pleasure in the orchard white,
Like nothing else by day, like ghosts by night;
And make us happy in the happy bees,
The swarm dilating round the perfect trees.

And make us happy in the darting bird
That suddenly above the bees is heard,
The meteor that thrusts in with needle bill,
And off a blossom in mid air stands still.

For this is love and nothing else is love,
The which it is reserved for God above
To sanctify to what far ends He will,
But which it only needs that we fulfill.

And then "The Impulse," from *Mountain Interval:*

"The Impulse"

It was too lonely for her there,
    And too wild,
And since there were but two of them,
    And no child,

And work was little in the house,
    She was free,
And followed where he furrowed field,
    Or felled tree.

She rested on a log and tossed
    The fresh chips,
With a song only to herself
    On her lips.

And once she went to break a bough
    Of black alder.
She strayed so far she scarcely heard
    When he called her—

And didn't answer—didn't speak—
    Or return.
She stood, and then she ran and hid
    In the fern.

He never found her, though he looked
    Everywhere,
And he asked at her mother's house
    Was she there.

Sudden and swift and light as that
    The ties gave,
And he learned of finalities
    Besides the grave.

And if this reading is followed by a reading of "The Axe-Helve"—with its half-formed thoughts, scarcely more than perplexed consciousness—it is possible to trace Mr. Frost's growth of interest in the experiences of folk whose lives are hard and dark and almost altogether physical.

The title poem of "New Hampshire"—more of which later—is not in the main current of this choice and development. One must turn to such poems as "The Star Splitter," "The Axe-Helve," "Paul's Wife," "Two Witches," and "A Fountain, a

Bottle, a Donkey's Ears and Some Books," to find the most graphic revelation of peculiar phenomena transpiring in queer chambers of consciousness.

Corresponding with these eccentric processes of thought and feeling as reported in the poems is the idiomatic quality in the medium. It is a medium frequently awkward in itself, sometimes even obscure, but suited to the business in hand. Familiarity with the New England country and its people is not, I think, a necessary circumstance to understanding the language and the thought and feeling back of it. Once I was present at a spirited controversy between two excellent critics as to the significance of Robert Frost—the one contending that [688] this poetry could make no claim to great and lasting art, because of its exceedingly provincial character, unintelligible to readers unfamiliar to the section, and the other answering with the names of Dante and Burns. It seemed to me then, and it seems to me now, that neither point of view touched the case of Frost with exactness. I cannot believe that a reader a thousand miles away and a hundred years hence would fail of Frost's meaning in the most colloquial of his poems. But neither do I think that this is because of the universality of human kinship in all essential feeling which renders Dante and Burns intelligible to any age and any country. George Moore's famous dictum that "Art, to become universal, must first be provincial," means, I think, not merely the obvious and fundamental truth that was in the mind of the second critic, but also that life—even where it is more or less isolated and individualized and peculiar—must be allowed to transpire in art in its own way and in its own language. We may count upon a certain universality of comprehension of life for life wherever it appears and with whatever eccentric gesture. The differences and divergencies are largely of degree and development, not of essence. All the potentialities are in every man.

All that has been said here has been on the subject of Frost as a poet of a restricted area and people—this, because it is that part of his poetry which gives him a striking and special significance in modern poetry, and because apparently it is upon that work that he and his readers place a conscious and calculating emphasis. But any view of his work which sees this, and only this, would exclude much that is moving and beautiful and that may be—who knows?—in the long wash of time, more lasting. In *A Boy's Will* is much that is fresh and lovely in youth's perennial reaction to the dewy world in which it finds itself set down.

There is nothing special or peculiar or eccentric about the feeling or its utterance, in the sense in which those words have been used of his New England poems. The same is true of some of the poems in the other volumes—"Putting in the Seed," "Loneliness" in *Mountain Interval*, and, curiously enough, even of more of the poems in *New Hampshire*. Certainly no special inheritance or environment is necessary for sharing in full the feeling of "Fragmentary Blue," with its beautiful clarity like morning light; or "Dust of Snow," or "Nothing Gold Can Stay." Here are poems of beautiful phrasing, whose feeling has no reference to environment or any other accidental circumstances. We are not accustomed to look to Frost for the complex element that is charm, but such poems as "The Runaway" and "Good-Bye and Keep Cold" have the intimacy of feeling and the unaffected grace of easy speech that invite another reading and another.

The title poem itself in *New Hampshire* is in line with neither of these departments of Mr. Frost's work, though it lies nearer to the New England character, of course. It is done with less seriousness, with a more whimsical and detached view of the people and the country. It is nearer to sublimated reporting than to high, interpretative poetry. At no time does the reader feel that the author is wholly identified with his theme—in the state of half-unconscious submersion in feeling which attends the creation of genius at its best. "New Hampshire" is interesting and brilliant. But one turns again to the vivid and telling revelation of New England life and character, and to the exquisite lyrics, referable to no locale or race, to be found elsewhere in the volume. [689]

❧ LOUIS UNTERMEYER ON *New Hampshire*[5]

It is somewhat more than seven years since Frost, following *North of Boston* with an equally characteristic though less integrated volume, published *Mountain Interval*. The latter work never succeeded to the popularity of its famous forerunner, and for no other reason but its very lack of unity. *North of Boston* presented a pattern—to many a dark and terrible pattern—in its interknit New England monologues; *Mountain Interval* scattered its effects, introduced new inflections, puzzled the admirers of Frost's "grey monotones" by an infusion of bright colors. Yet some of this poet's finest moments are in the lesser known book. Nothing from the more popular collection will last longer than the dramatically suspended "Snow," the idyllic "Birches," or the intensity of the "Hill Wife" lyrics; even "The Death of the Hired Man" scarcely surpasses the charged pathos of "An Old Man's Winter Night."

And now, after seven years, we have *New Hampshire* which, structurally, is a cross between both its predecessors. With an almost equal division of narratives and lyrics, it seems to recall *Mountain Interval,* but the unity of *North of Boston* is achieved by a peculiar and simple device. *New Hampshire* pretends to be nothing but a long poem with notes and grace notes, and the title poem (some fourteen pages long) purports merely to celebrate Frost's favorite state. Very gravely, the rambling tribute to the state that "hasn't much of anything to sell" is starred and dotted with scientific numerals in the manner of the most profound treatise, the references being to poems that look at first as if they were only inserted to reenforce the text. In reality, these explanatory "notes" are some of the richest poems of our time, poems steeped in that extraordinary blend of intellect and emotion which is Frost's particular magic. Thus the tiny numeral after the line:

> She has one witch—old style[1]

[5] "Robert Frost's *New Hampshire*," *Bookman* (New York), LVIII (January 1924), 578-580.

refers us to [1] "The Witch of Coös," one of the most singularly related ghost stories in poetry. Thus, another strange narrative is introduced in this way:

> I met a Californian who would
> Talk California—a state so blessed,
> He said, in climate, none had ever died there
> A natural death, and Vigilance Committees
> Had had to organize to stock the graveyards[2]
> And vindicate the state's humanity.
> "Just the way Stefansson runs on," I murmured,
> "About the British Arctic. That's what comes
> Of being in the market with a climate."

[2] Cf. page 51, "Place for a Third."

But is it a different poet that breaks silence after seven years with so unusual an arrangement? Will the admirers of the earlier Frost fail to find him in this strange composition? [578] Frost himself might answer with the words of the first poem in his first book:

> They would not find me changed from him they knew—
> Only more sure of all I thought was true.

Nothing, really, has changed. The idiom is clearer, the convictions have deepened—the essential things, the point of view, the tone of voice, remain the same. . . .

What change there is, is one of emphasis. It seems incredible that most of the appraisers of Frost's previous work spoke chiefly of its grimness, whereas its whimsicality, though less obvious, was equally pronounced. In *Mountain Interval*, the occasional quizzical raillery of *North of Boston* was more apparent, the momentary descent of the eyelash was perceptibly prolonged; in *New Hampshire* it declares itself on every page. The very form of the new book is an extended piece of badinage; the long title poem is a broad smile from beginning to end; the most serious of the narratives sparkle with a slily intimate banter. This increase in humor, so rich in its varying timbres, [579] will irritate the literal minded almost as much as it will delight those to whom fact and fantasy are not inimical opposites but continually shifting facets of the same many sided thing. The orthodox Cam-

bridgian (Mass.), for example, will boil over at such an outrageous heresy as:

> Her husband was worth millions.
> I think he owned some shares in Harvard College.

The critics who concluded that Frost was too overburdened
with his lonely farms and isolated cottages, who maintained that
he could never be "whimsical or quaint," will scarcely know
what to make of this volume in which practically every poem
proceeds from a magnified whimsicality. There will be those
who, granting the charm of this elfin imagination, may question
its use in such serious themes. Yet what is poetry but metaphor
—what is it but the establishing of a congruity between apparently unrelated things? What then is metaphor but the child of
whimsy?

So much has been made of Frost's factual realism that at the
risk of being redundant I insist that, beneath the surface natural-
ism, his work is distinguished—even impelled—by a rare and
fantastic mind. This side of Frost's genius has been so under-
emphasized that I may be allowed to overstress it by directing
attention to the fundamental quaintness of conception of "Paul's
Wife," the extraordinarily adroit "An Empty Threat," "A Star
in a Stone-Boat," that lovely chain of tercets, and "Wild Grapes,"
which is a feminine complement to "Birches."

But it is in the lyrics that Frost's warmth is most apparent.
There are few circumlocutory asides, few *sotto voce* murmurs,
in these direct communications—only a firm intensity. A great
love of the New England countryside, of earth itself, surges from
such poems as "Stopping By Woods on a Snowy Evening,"
"Gathering Leaves," "In a Disused Graveyard," and the brightly
ironic "The Need of Being Versed in Country Things." A less
physical and almost unearthly passion speaks in the beautiful
though troubled lines of "To Earthward," the mystical sonority
of "I Will Sing You One-O," and the condensed wisdom of
"Fire and Ice." I consider the last, one of the greatest epigram-
matic poems in the English language; every line—and there are
only nine altogether—seems to have been carved in crystal. Simi-
larly concentrated, though in far lighter accents, is this perfectly
balanced composition ["Nothing Gold Can Stay"]. It seems so
spontaneous and integrated a song that it is interesting to note that

the first six lines were composed a score of years ago, Frost
having waited twenty years for the last two.

> Nature's first green is gold,
> Her hardest hue to hold.
> Her early leaf's a flower;
> But only so an hour.
> Then leaf subsides to leaf.
> So Eden sank to grief,
> So dawn goes down to day.
> Nothing gold can stay.

In the very simplicity of these lines we have the unaffected
originality of Frost. With absolute freedom from contemporary
fashions, technical trickery, or the latest erudite slang, Frost has
created a poetry which is at one time full of heat and humor, a
poetry that belongs not only to the America of our own day but
to the richest records of English verse. [580]

❦ ISIDOR SCHNEIDER ON *Collected Poems*[6]

A reading of the *Collected Poems* can leave no doubt of Mr.
Frost's importance. They have an appearance of obscurity, but
what renders them difficult to first reading renders them also
powerful and compact. The simplicity of their subject matter is
never betrayed into coarseness or sentimentality. They constitute
a body of poetry certain to enter into classic American literature.

However, since current reviews of this volume are all praise
and no serious criticism is being attempted, I think it may be of
interest to point out the limiting elements in Mr. Frost's work.
There is a danger in too complete an acceptance of any man's
achievement, a possibility of his influence becoming a catch-all
for literary prejudice.

Mr. Frost, for instance, is singularly out of touch with his
own time. Indeed, many poets who antedate him are more contemporary in spirit. It has, indeed, been Mr. Frost's wish to keep
out of his own age and his own civilization. We may go therefore
to his poetry for diversion and relief from our time, but not for

---

[6] "Robert Frost," *Nation*, CXXXII (January 28, 1931), 101-102.

illumination. Mr. Frost does not understand our time and will make no effort to understand it. When he essays to speak of it, as in the long poem "New Hampshire" (one of the poorest in the book and a sort of pudding of irrelevancies), he shows a surprising lack of comprehension. There, to the challenge of contemporary ideas, he replies with know-nothing arrogance, "Me for the hills where I don't have to choose."

In fact, Mr. Frost's work is weakest in ideas. His style is gnomic; it sounds impressively thoughtful and many sentences have the rounded conclusiveness of proverbs. But his thought, disengaged from the style, is often discovered to be no thought at all, or a banality. (I am far from agreeing with Mr. George Moore and other advocates of "pure poetry" that ideas are foreign to the nature of poetry. Shakespeare, Dante, Goethe, Milton, Donne, Lucretius would have to be among the many poets sacrificed, and the purification of poetry would turn out to be its annihilation.) Mr. Frost has casual ambitions to be a philosopher in his poetry; and in these strivings he is not successful.

We may take for example the beautiful poem "A Star in a Stone Boat." The star is a meteorite built into a stone wall. Mr. Frost follows it from its fall to the time a farmer finds it, handles it, puts it into a stone boat, and drags it to the wall he is building. We are given a marvelous sense of its weight and feel in the hands and the puzzled awe with which one looks at it. The concluding lines are perfect:

> Such as it is, it promises the prize
> Of the one world complete in any size
> That I am like to compass, fool or wise.

These lines, summarizing as much of philosophy as the poem comes to, do not contain thought so much as a renunciation of thought. I doubt whether a poet of philosophic imagination could have given us a more satisfying poem. Nevertheless, this piece, so suggestive and so full of possibilities, shows how little the philosophic imagination is developed in Mr. Frost.

It is curious, therefore, that Mr. Frost should be so regularly praised for the thought content of his poetry. But there is a reason for it. The touch of philosophy in his writing is the commonest, most easily understood, most easily applied, most comforting form of thinking—renunciation. Mr. Frost adds to it no subtlety and no depths; when it occurs in his poems it is, despite the graces and novelties of his style, banality. [101]

I dwell upon this because it is the one respect in which Mr. Frost clearly shows himself to be influenced. The influence is New England, the New England of other days. The individuality of his style is one of the valuable effects of this influence, for New England life and tradition have always encouraged intense individualism. But this individualism derives in part from renunciation. What a man renounces he is free from and in freedom he can be himself. Perhaps here lies an explanation of the individuality of Mr. Frost's style. He has made a renunciation of usual poetic subject matter and usual poetic effects, not primarily for originality's sake, but in disdain of literary comforts. He has chosen instead to write of homely and country things, regarding them with his matchlessly keen observation and celebrating them with his almost painfully restrained eloquence. No doubt some deliberate and unnecessarily harsh lines are a further process of this renunciation.

Related to this lack of a developed and original philosophy is another lack. Mr. Frost's narrative poems are frequently poised upon a psychological situation. The satisfaction the poetry and the narrative give the reader often leaves him with the impression that Mr. Frost is an excellent psychologist. Now many poets have been good psychologists, as Freud has shown; but Mr. Frost as a psychologist does not get very far. He can describe sensations perfectly; in fact, such descriptions are among his finest achievements. But he does not reach beyond the sensation; and in a psychological narrative he does not reach beyond the fact. The interesting poem of the man who burned down his house to buy a telescope with the insurance money succeeds only in reporting a curiosity; the poem "Maple," which attempts to describe the psychological effects of having an unusual name, stretches out to absurd length in the attempt and succeeds in doing no more than to supply the reader data for his own psychologizing.

No, the distinctions Mr. Frost achieves are not those of a thinker or a prober; nor does he need those. He has rounded out a poetic individuality of exceptional dignity; he has developed his descriptive powers to an accuracy so sensitive that his lines often have an effect of clairvoyance; and the patient, logical fulfilment of his metaphors gives his rhetoric an effectiveness achieved by very few poets besides him.

Mr. Frost's style is one of the most individual in all poetry and certainly the most individual of our time. The consciously aristocratic T. S. Eliot, with his almost selfish obscurities, the dazzlingly inventive E. E. Cummings, with all his inimitable experiments, sound like the generality beside him. It is impossible to describe this individuality because its most conspicuous elements, terseness and the use of plain words and the avoidance of metronomic rhythms, are characteristics of many other poets. One can only say that Mr. Frost writes in a manner wholly his own; and if he has been influenced in it at all, it is only in the individualism urged by the New England tradition.

The descriptive power of Mr. Frost is to me the most wonderful thing in his poetry. A snowfall, a spring thaw, a bending tree, a valley mist, a brook, these are brought not to, but into the experience of the reader. The method is simple and can be analyzed. What he describes is never a spectacle only, but an entire adventure. In "Our Singing Strength" we follow him disputing with birds a bit of roadway; in "A Hillside Thaw" we almost see him on his knees trying to feel with his hands the process of snow turning into water. With the sight and the act the emotional response comes naturally. The three fuse together and the experience comes whole to us. It is an effect rare even in the best poetry. This simultaneous description gives the reader almost a sensory instrument with which to share the perception; and since it is natural, anyway, for the reader to identify himself with the author, the result is to bring the reader into closer touch with this aloof poet than with many poets who directly seek such a companionship.

Metaphors as Mr. Frost uses them are more functional than they commonly are in poetry. Many poets have more abundance and more brilliance, but few have used metaphor so justly, so carefully, and so fully. It is worked in naturally and at length, becoming a part of the whole idea, not a mere illuminating flash. The most conspicuous example of this is "A Hillside Thaw." The first three lines announce the metaphor.

> To think to know the country and not know
> The hillside on the day the sun lets go
> Ten million silver lizards out of snow!

For most poets this would be sufficient. They would turn to other metaphors. But Mr. Frost continues it for thirty-two lines more, and we have a wonderfully complete sense of the coolness, swiftness, and liquidness of these snow lizards that the night will catch and hold, and the sun will again release in the next daylight.

There remains to make some estimate among the poems themselves. The later sections are much superior to the earlier, where the poems are frequently incomplete, beginning with promises of drama, of discoveries of thought that fail into unresolved and weak endings. This disappears in the later poems which, with the exception of the poem "New Hampshire," are sound throughout. On the whole it seems to me that the longer lyrics are the most thoroughly satisfying of his poems. The narratives, although among the best in English poetry, suffer from the incompatibility found in all narrative poetry which attempts to be realistic—the rivalry of the poetic and the colloquial. The attempt to fuse the two seems to me doomed to failure; a noble failure, preferable to easier successes, but a failure nevertheless. It were better for a narrative poem to be written wholly in poetic language, which, being complete and self-sufficient in its own terms, will sound natural, certainly more natural than when colloquialisms are inset and draw attention to their competing naturalness. A few of the very short lyrics in the book are inconsequential and, as in "Fireflies in the Garden," tend to become cute. Mr. Frost seems to require space to express himself, for in a few lines his terseness and involution have the look of a mannerism.

In conclusion I wish to say again outright in words what I have already said by implication—Robert Frost is one of the great poets, one whose perceptions are among the most acute and the most personal in the whole range of literature. To this nearly every one of the poems written in his maturity bears witness.
[102]

WILLIAM ROSE BENÉT ON *A Further Range*[7]

Two American poets of my time have possessed an integrity they wore so easily that no one could imagine them being otherwise. One is dead, Edwin Arlington Robinson, and one—we thank the gods—is still alive and writing with the same felicity and shrewd wisdom as of old. Of what does such integrity consist? One would say the chief element is being oneself. But then one really has to be someone in the first place. We soon find out what a man can do and how well he does it. But in the case of a major writer, the whole life becomes involved in the work. No matter how reticent he may be, or how objectively he may write, the whole man comes before us. A certain voice is speaking that is like no other. And that is not because he decides to adopt certain characteristics of style. His style grows out of his way of thinking and speaking. The commonplace, the specious, never achieve style. And no form of writing more betrays a man than the practice of what we call poetry.

Frost, I think, is a major poet, because he is, for one thing, a significant human being. He is definitely one certain kind of human being and has his own limitations; but he early decided to be his own man, and by so being he has developed his own special gift to the full. Probably there has only been one poet in the whole history of the world who could be all things to all men, and that was Shakespeare. Compared with that extraordinary phenomenon all other poets are minor, though all those we call major had their special gifts. But there is no use putting people into a pantheon too early, and it is of no particular importance, save to say that here is an American of whom we can rightly be proud as we are proud of Emerson, and that to me is saying a great deal.

But Frost is no transcendentalist. He is a close observer of the earth and the ways of man on the earth. When he first came into his own and wrote the line about "the highway where the slow wheel pours the sand" he demonstrated that he had the god-given

[7] "Wise Old Woodchuck," *Saturday Review of Literature*, XIV (May 30, 1936), 6.

faculty of reporting as a poet—of all beings at his best the most accurate—precisely what he saw. We have got used to that now, got used to his constantly opening our eyes to the things we overlook that he clothes with significance. He came before us quietly, with no blatancy, no fanfare, and at first we may have thought—we who were so romantic and so dramatic then—that it was commonplace. But how well he wears! No fuss and feathers. Just a man we like to listen to, because wisdom out of deep experience wells through his words.

So what?—says the young poet—you would have me become an admirable character first and all things poetic shall be added unto me? Unfortunately not. I am not forgetting the man of a craft. I suppose a thorough rascal might yet be a good stone-mason. That is a craft. So is verse. Frost is a craftsman of verse. But when verse somehow becomes poetry it certainly implies that you are not a rascal; at least, not a thorough one. Frost is a bit of a rascal at that. I think he is a bit of a rascal for being so intensely individual. But it is only that kind of rascality that gives tang to a man's work.

> Only where love and need are one,
> And the work is play for mortal stakes,
> Is the deed ever really done
> For Heaven and the future's sakes.

And what does he say in the brevities of "Ten Mills"?

["Pertinax"]

> Let chaos storm!
> Let cloud shapes swarm!
> I wait for form.

At a time of the most extravagant experimentation in verse, that is the craftsman speaking. No, young poet, you must learn the trade and how to use the tools! But brilliant as your performance then may be, behind it must be your own stature. Make no mistake about that! Nor, it has been doubted, is a cubit added merely by taking thought. But don't involve me in metaphysics!

> They cannot look out far.
> They cannot look in deep.
> But when was that ever a bar
> To any watch they keep?

When we find a man who can look out far and look in deep, and at the same time express himself clearly, to say that we should be grateful is understatement.

Frost's way of writing sometimes looks so easy; it is only when you examine it closely and note the careful use of every word, which has now become second nature, and the way he has of stating anything with inimitable idiosyncrasy, that despair sets in. There have been some pretty good imitators, but they have not got far.

Why should I tell you what is in this new book? Read it! It is a small book, as books go; it is actually only the sixth book we have had from a man now with so large a reputation. And it is better worth reading than nine-tenths of the books that will come your way this year. In a time when all kinds of insanity are assailing the nations it is good to listen to this quiet humor, even about a hen, a hornet, or Square Matthew. Frost, as woodchuck, has been "instinctively thorough" about his burrow. Perhaps that is all it was from the first. Yet he has not only burrowed deep but sat often at the burrow-mouth to watch the great drift of the constellations. Wise old woodchuck! And if he has not got the whole "United States stated," he has got a good deal of life stated in original analogy and phrase. And if anybody should ask me why I still believe in my land, I have only to put this book in his hand and answer, "Well—here is a man of my country."
[6]

✿ DUDLEY FITTS ON *A Further Range*[8]

It is difficult to approach this book quite fairly. If only it were a first book, or if Frost's earlier work were less consistent in mood and technic, appraisal would be easier. As it is, one is distracted by a pre-established Frost manner: one expects certain idiosyncrasies of phrasing and diction, the texture apparently loose yet actually cunningly woven, the careful and felicitous

[8] Untitled review, *New England Quarterly*, IX (September 1936), 519-521.

colloquialism of tone, and consequently one is in danger of judging these poems not for themselves alone, but in the light of a preconceived notion of what they should be and what they should do. Accordingly, a good poem may seem invalid only because there is nothing in the manner to account for it; and a weak poem may achieve an apparent success because it evokes the glamour of a remembered excellence.

To be specific: one is perfectly at home with the short lyrics, such poems as "After-flakes," "Lost in Heaven," the fine "A Blue Ribbon at Amesbury," or "Desert Places." Here is Frost at his purest and best: no one else writes in this way, no one else has ever written precisely in this way. The quality is vibrant, eager, and curiously young; it is pure incantation, the more moving because it is managed by the simplest and homeliest [519] means. In the same tradition are many of the longer, more dramatic pieces: "The Gold Hesperidee," for instance, and "The Old Barn at the Bottom of the Fogs." If these poems are generally less distinguished than the lyrics, it is because they are discursive, and because they more easily admit two elements which have marred much of Frost's work for at least one of his readers: an obvious didacticism, and a ponderous kind of playfulness.

It is in the long poems at the end of the book, however, that we encounter something unexpected. It is an extended statement of an attitude that has been only implicit before: a social attitude, satirically and most ambitiously exploited in "Build Soil— A Political Pastoral." And it is precisely here, where one would naturally have looked for the strongest writing, that the manner seems to break down completely. The voice is still the voice of Frost, it is true, and all the tricks are here; but the diction is faded, the expression imprecise, and the tone extraordinarily tired and uneasy. It is a strange thing that Robert Frost, pondering the problem of a sick society, should suddenly become ineffectual, should seem unable to deal abstractly with matters that he has powerfully suggested in many of his best lyrics. It is almost as though he had taken one of those incomparable lyrics—say "A Blue Ribbon at Amesbury," where much is implied—and drawn its essence out into an extended "message" poem, a diluted form of

Thanks, thanks to thee, my worthy friend,
For the lesson thou hast taught.

It is not that his social attitude suggests nothing new: is something new demanded? The trouble is that it suggests nothing at all so much as a man who wishes he had never brought up the subject in the first place. Whatever the reason, the "Political Pastoral," and three or four pieces like it, elaborate a quality hitherto not to be found in Frost: a sterility.

It is as a lyrist in a special field that Frost is supreme, and *A Further Range* is a book of the greatest distinction in so far as it is a reaffirmation of a standard already established. Among two or three poems of exceptional beauty the shortest and the finest of them all deserves to be quoted: [520]

"Moon Compasses"

I stole forth dimly in the dripping pause
Between two downpours to see what there was.
And a masked moon had spread down compass rays
To a cone mountain in the midnight haze,
As if the final estimate were hers,
And as it measured in her calipers,
The mountain stood exalted in its place.
So love will take between the hands a face. . . .

Is this not the fatal note of the great poetry? *Cedite Romani scriptores, cedite Graii!* [521]

❧ JOHN WHEELWRIGHT ON *A Further Range*[9]

Upon the eve of Robinson's fame, some spoke of Frost in the same breath; and now Robinson is dead, Frost is our leading poet. His fame shall rest upon a firmer basis. Robinson, like MacLeish, can be judged not so much by his work as by why people like it, whereas with Frost the audience [45] counts less than the good work. He has never been able to be as boring as Robinson's most boring; his best is beyond Robinson's best.

But not so far beyond as one might expect from this "heir

---

9 "Back to the Old Farm," *Poetry*, XLIX (October 1936), 45-48.

to New England"; that is, to Transcendentalism; that is, to Emerson. Emerson cut Frost's work out for him (*Hamatreya* and *Earth-Song*). Frost has not bettered the pattern. He is not a transcendental but an allegorical poet: "Thought is round," he says, but thought is spiral. Nor is he exactly Yankee, but rather a common American returned Eastward upon the Westward track. He comes not *off of* the Farm, but *back to* the Farm. Sick sign in body politic, his thought is pastoral.

A shiftlessness which city men gone rustic take on as country character because they are not born and bred to function in a farm's ordered disorder is the characteristic of Frost's work. With slip-shod affectation grown to natural grace, occasionally slovenly, it has habitual style, and anyhow when he drops it for urbane neatness, as in a half dozen of the poems now under review, he appears with the natty things of the small townsman turned hay-seed back in town.

Thought matters more than style, though the one go with the other. Frost, a didactic poet, says in a political dialogue, "Let me preach to you, will you, Meliboeus?" and answers, "Preach on. I thought you were already preaching. But preach, and let me see if I can tell the difference." What a difference, once he lets on what he has been putting over [46] all these years—the lure of subsistence farming as catch-pool spiritual and temporal! So long as his teaching is only a record of observation, the observation seems accurate so far as the record goes. And it goes further with longer sight. But once presented sententiously, to be "Taken Doubly" or "Taken Singly" in "range beyond range even into the realm of government and religion," how thin, how two-dimensional! Poems with some spread in meaning simply do not hold the philosophic weight and strain they are put under. The Bard turns simpleton.

Cage himself about as he will; warn us, "Don't let the things I say against myself Betray you into taking sides against me Or it might get you into trouble with me"; brag as he will that like a Pickwick wood-chuck he digs a two-door burrow; sings "Back to the Farm," but not so 16 million unemployed may hear;—with all this he is shrewishly saying: We don't *like* Socialism in our house, because Socialism is just Capitalism turned up-side-down, and we don't *like* Capitalism. And then he turns out a revolutionary poem to show that Foxy Grandpa is not really snoozing.

Frost's good work is beyond his audience. His other work is beneath them. As Robinson was a favorite with Theodore Roosevelt, Frost at his worst is a poetic Calvin Coolidge for the Herbert Hoovers. Rugged Individuals! Join the United States! Nay, worse, he is the laureate of the New Deal. Take him politically to heart and you further the darkest (because the least frank) reaction. His Five-Year [47] Plan (yes, he has one, too) of one-man strikes against Gold and Invention will never further any distant objective he holds out as an ideal, nor embarrass that Greed which he scolds about so irresponsibly and which is our salvation yet. His Conservatism vs. Radicalism is a half-toasted substitute for half-baked bread.

The trouble is he does not practice what he preaches. Where Voltaire advised, "Till your soil," Frost advises: "Turn the crop under." Good advice. Frost condemns our over-extended economy, but he is beyond contempt in smug approbation of mere subsistence living and on all counts reprehensible in not turning under his own crop of green ideas to enrich his own soil. A good individualist, he has over-extended himself.

A Further Range is a peculiarly youthful book. If an unpublished poet submitted it and the book before it to a publisher's reader, the conscientious report would be that half of each, backed up by two or three more books, would show a poet to be mentioned in the same breath with Robinson; and then, now Robinson is dead, Frost would be our leading poet.

He holds his own because he is distinct among all his rivals and because a teeming welter of talent, finer in prosody and firmer in philosophy, is so indistinct by reason of keen rivalry that no critic has picked any one poet to match against Robert Frost. [48]

❧ J. H. JOHNSTON ON *Complete Poems*[10]

Since Robert Frost has reached some stature and maturity in contemporary American literature, the latest collection of his poetry affords a range of craftsmanship and thought solid enough

---

[10] Untitled review in *Commonweal*, L (July 8, 1949), 324-325.

and complete enough for some tentative re-estimations, not only of Frost himself, but of the American mentality—both popular and academic—which has acclaimed him as a poet of talent and as a man of original educative wisdom.

From the sharp and simple imagery of Frost's best lyrics, to the flippant crowing in "New Hampshire," "Build Soil," and *A Masque of Reason*, is a distance that cannot be accounted for by a perversion of talent: for the poet's bucolic canniness, his contempt for the "intellectual," and his hard appraisal of systematized knowledge and values, often intersects with the cleanest lyrical vision. Frost's geographic regionalism—almost all of his poetry has originated in New England—is matched by a psychological and spiritual regionalism of a pernicious sort. "The fact is the sweetest dream that labor knows" is a sentiment that Americans have popularly recognized as their own, just as they have recognized, and responded to, all sentiments of presentism and practicality from Franklin onward. But the insistence on the fact and on the rough realities of New England farming life in Frost's poetry, combines curiously with a disavowal [324] of the responsibilities of a common intellectual and social heritage; both combine, still more curiously, with a romantic and often sentimental mystique, a coagulate of stars, snow and birch-trees. From all of this is derived a vague but strongly individualistic moral theology, by turns shrewdly practical and whimsically impractical.

Frost's achievement in clean lyrical poetry is considerable; but if his songs are pressed (as all songs should be pressed) they often reveal a disturbing indetermination and shallowness. [325]

❧ ROLFE HUMPHRIES ON *Complete Poems*[11]

So here are the *Complete Poems*, to date, at least, of Robert Frost (Henry Holt, $6). With the volume in hand, knowing the poems, knowing also what one knows, or thinks one knows, or has heard about the poet aside from the poems, one hesitates to open the pages, indulging, first, in a little utterly idle speculation. What would have happened had Frost gone off on some road

---

[11] "Verse Chronicle," *Nation*, CLXIX (July 23, 1949), 92-93.

not taken? Suppose, for instance, he had spent his years of growth, or his artistic maturity, not in New England, nor old England, either, but Ireland or France, Paris or Dublin. Suppose he had had his native simile jarred, suppose he had knocked around in, and been knocked around by, the company of his peers, with a ribald Gogarty or a wild old wicked Yeats, a Verlaine, a Rimbaud, a Baudelaire, looking over his shoulder or arguing far into the night. Up to a point, I think, no one would want Frost different: it is when his paths diverge, and he chooses, not one of two ways, but two at once, that one regrets the split, the waste of energy, the element of denial.

Creatively, there are at least three Frosts—the actual artist, the legendary public character, posed and professed, and the latent, potential poet that might have been. The fellow in the middle, it must be said to his credit, has interfered very little with the first; he has, however, I think, considerably stunted the growth of the last. Everybody knows, and too many admire, this character, the local wiseacre, rural sage, town whittler, Will Rogers and Cal Coolidge combined, village idiot (in the Greek sense of the noun). To a sophisticated, Alexandrian, professional, academic, middle-class, urban audience, this version of pastoral has great appeal; we do not see too clearly how much it is of the bourgeois, by the bourgeois, for the bourgeois. This is the side of Frost that speaks for the first time, and for the first time with smugness, in the title poem of the collection called *New Hampshire*, his fourth book and one which contains some of his finest work; it is occasionally heard thereafter, intermittently, the slightest soupçon, in *West-Running Brook*, becomes a good deal more insistent in *A Further Range*, culminating in the ugly editorials in *Steeple Bush*, and the arch gerontic garrulities and mock sapience of the two masques. On this side of Frost it is not very pleasant to dwell.

As actual artist Frost has won double triumph, in fields which would seem to lie far enough apart so that a conqueror seldom invades both with success. There is the fine and beautiful lyric poetry—"Reluctance" in *A Boy's Will*; "The Road Not Taken," "The Sound of the Trees," in *Mountain Interval*; "Fire and Ice," "In a Disused Graveyard," "Stopping by Woods on a Snowy Evening," in *New Hampshire*; "Bereft," "Acquainted with the Night," in *West-Running Brook*; "Come In," in *A Further*

Range; "A Nature Note," in *A Witness Tree*—these are not all, only the most conspicuous that can be cited.

What is not so often found in the lyric poet is the ability to turn outward, to manage the modes of speech as well as those of song, to be dramatic as well as personal, to get out of the self and into insight into the selves of others. No single adjective, like lyric, can be found to apply to this side of Frost's excellence—what shall we say, dramatic monologue, bucolic idyl, epyllion, to describe those somewhat longer poems of Frost's, so many of which are so good? "The Death of the Hired Man," almost all the poems in *North of Boston* (one or two are flops, to be sure, for example "A Hundred Collars," but there are interesting elements even in the unsuccessful items); "Out, Out" and "Snow," in *Mountain Interval*, the first missing melodrama, perhaps, only by its terrible brevity and economy; "The Witch of Coös" in *New Hampshire*—what can be said about poems like these is that they stand with Chaucer's and Browning's, a little less in good cheer and gusto, and a little more in sensitive and reserved compassion. And the ear for speech as superlative as Lardner's. [92]

To have succeeded in two areas as diverse as these would seem to be almost enough for one man to have accomplished, and I was going to rest my case there, but I find, as I run through the pages, another kind of poem that I cannot resist delighting in and praising. That would be the kind of poem that uses, mainly, the cadence and line of the ones mentioned in the paragraph above, and devotes itself to observation, of nature, or occupation, with a little commentary, humorous, it may be, or semi-rueful: "After Apple-Picking" is a case in point, "An Old Man's Winter Night," that wonderful accuracy of "The Grindstone," "A Hillside Thaw," "The Runaway," the middle stanza of "The White-Tailed Hornet." Some of the dogmatism in "Two Tramps in Mud Time" gets my back up, but who could resist:

> Good blocks of oak it was I split,
> As large around as the chopping-block;
> And every piece I squarely hit
> Fell splinterless as a cloven rock. . . .
>
> The sun was warm but the wind was chill.
> You know how it is with an April day
> When the sun is out and the wind is still,

74

You're one month on in the middle of May.
But if you so much as dare to speak,
A cloud comes over the sunlit arch,
A wind comes off a frozen peak,
And you're two months back in the middle of March.

Well: and after all this, Frost being this good, how dare anyone be disappointed in him, or wish him to have been better? A fair question, however difficult, and deserving a serious answer. In a way the dissatisfaction is the compliment; Frost himself all through his work, more or less, offers clues as to the kind of thing he might have done, the line of a frightful and fascinating interest that he almost dared to follow. The road not taken. "Here error is all in the not done/all in the diffidence that faltered"—Frost states the case, for (and against) himself:

> The bearer of evil tidings
> When he was halfway there,
> Remembered that evil tidings
> Were a dangerous thing to bear.

Frost has been halfway there, or farther, much more than once: as early as "The Fear," in *North of Boston*, as late as "The Subverted Flower," in *A Witness Tree*—and there are other poems which show where he has turned off the woodland trail, briefly, toward the heart of some deeper forest, jungle, sinister tarn—"Fire and Ice," "The Bonfire," "The Lockless Door," "Bereft," "The Lovely Shall Be Choosers," with its cadences broken, out of dreams, and here and there very frightening, "Desert Places," "The Rabbit Hunter," "The Night Light," "Design." Reading such poems as these, one cannot escape the impression that they are much more truly the essence of the poet than the plain New Hampshire farmer is, or Meliboeus the potato man, or whoever; one wishes he had been a little less fearful of evil tidings, less scared of his own desert places. One wishes he had wasted less time being sane and wholesome, and gone really all out, farther than he did beyond the boundaries of New England's quaintness into its areas of violence, madness, murder, rape, and incest (for *New England's* read *humanity's*). "Any eye is an evil eye/that looks in on to a mood apart"; the heart of man is desperately wicked; I (read Everyman) am a villain. It is this night side of life and nature that Frost's art has, I think, scamped reporting, and not because he did not know it; no American poet in our time, no American poet, nor Poe in his stories, has come closer to Baudelaire. [93]

❦ PETER VIERECK ON *Complete Poems*[12]

An unusual variety of new books of poetry has appeared in recent months. In a comparative reading several superlatives suggest themselves. The most important book of 1949 is the *Complete Poems of Robert Frost* (Holt). It is—to make a point-blank value-judgment—the year's "best" by any American poet. . . .

Robert Frost's name is rarely heard among the exquisites of *avant-garde*. His poems are like those plants that flourish in the earth of the broad plains and valleys but will not strike root in more rarefied atmospheres. The fact remains that he is one of the world's greatest living poets. Frost, W. H. Auden, Wallace Stevens, and William Carlos Williams are the contemporary poets in America whose styles are most intensely original, most unmistakably their own. Of the four, Frost is the only one to be widely read in terms of general circulation and the only one who has never been adequately subjected to the Higher Criticism of the *doctores subtiles* of the Little Magazines.

On first reading, Frost seems easier than he really is. This helps account both for the enormous number of his readers, some of whom like him for wrong or irrelevant reasons, and for the indifference of the coteries, who become almost resentful when they can find no double-crostics to solve. Frost's cheerfulness is often mistaken as smug, folksy, Rotarian. This fact, plus his reputation for a solid New England conservatism, frightens away rebel youth and "advanced" professors. [67]

In truth, his cheerfulness is the direct opposite of Mr. Babbitt's or even of Mr. Pickwick's. It is a Greek cheerfulness. And the apparent blandness of the Greeks was, as Nietzsche showed in his *Birth of Tragedy*, the result of their having looked so deeply into life's tragic meaning that they had to protect themselves by

[12] From "Parnassus Divided," *Atlantic Monthly*, CLXXXIV (October 1949), 67-70.

cultivating a deliberately superficial jolliness in order to bear the unbearable. Frost's benign calm, the cosmic mask of a whittling rustic, is designed for gazing—without dizziness—into a tragic abyss of desperation. This is the same eternal abyss that gaped not only for the Hellenes but for such moderns as Pascal, Kierkegaard, Nietzsche, Baudelaire, Kafka. "Pascal," wrote Baudelaire, "had his abyss that followed him." In the case of this great New England tragic poet, the desperation is no less real for being a quiet one, as befits a master of overwhelming understatements. His almost too smooth quietness is a booby trap to spring the ruthless doubt of the following typical Frostian quatrain:—

> It was the drought of deserts. Earth would soon
> Be uninhabitable as the moon.
> What for that matter had it ever been?
> Who advised man to come and live therein?

Or ponder upon the following four lines, where again the meaning sneaks up on you imperceptibly and leaves a sense of ephemeral human smallness in the eons it takes for the sun to burn out:—

The play seems out for an almost infinite run.
Don't mind a little thing like the actors fighting.
The only thing I worry about is the sun.
We'll be all right if nothing goes wrong with the lighting.

Or this:—

> A voice said, Look me in the stars
> And tell me truly, men of earth,
> If all the soul-and-body scars
> Were not too much to pay for birth.

Let those who consider Frost obvious or superficial brood a bit upon the last line of "Never Again Would Birds' Song Be the Same." Consisting only of simple monosyllables yet subtly musical and full of "the shock of recognition," that concluding sentence is perhaps the most beautiful single line in American literature, a needed touchstone for all poets writing today:—

> He would declare and could himself believe
> That the birds there in all the garden round
> From having heard the daylong voice of Eve
> Had added to their own an oversound,

Her tone of meaning but without the words.

. . . .

Moreover her voice upon their voices crossed
Had now persisted in the woods so long
That probably it never would be lost.
Never again would birds' song be the same.
And to do that to birds was why she came.

Many writers have described nature's brutal threat to mankind, but rarely with so strong a metaphor as Frost's description of the hills of earth in "Sand Dunes":—

Sea waves are green and wet,
But up from where they die,
Rise others vaster yet,
And those are brown and dry.

They are the sea made land
To come at the fisher town,
And bury in solid sand
The men she could not drown.

But the poem ends with hope, for man remains free to think. This hope is based not on the pollyanna of easy optimism but on the tragic wisdom of those who through the ages have not only stared into the abyss but have outstared it. This is probably the final message of Frost's *Complete Poems*.

A word about his metrics and his diction. Frost is one of the few poets today who dare use contractions like "as 'twere" and "e'er." I don't care for this sort of thing, especially in a poet who makes a point of catching the idiom of everyday speech. But I don't let this annoying anachronism spoil my enjoyment of him. Equally old-fashioned, but this time in a better sense of the word, is the fact that his meters scan with a beat-by-beat regularity, usually in the form of rhymed iambic pentameters. In this connection, do not overlook his thoughtful preface on poetic techniques and meters.

Frost's stubborn conventionality of form makes many young poets and readers think his is also a conventionality of meaning. On the contrary, he is one of the most original writers of our time. It is the self-conscious *avant-garde* rebels who follow the really rigid and tiresome conventions. [68]

✿ FROST ON POETRY

✦✦-✦✦-✦✦-✦✦-✦✦-✦✦-✦✦-✦✦-✦✦-✦✦-✦✦-✦✦-✦✦-✦✦-✦✦-✦✦-

✿ FROM "EDUCATION BY POETRY:
A MEDITATIVE MONOLOGUE"[1]

How shall a man go through college without having been marked for taste and judgment? What will become of him? What will his end be? He will have to take continuation courses for college graduates. He will have to go to night schools. They are having night schools now, you know, for college graduates. Why? Be- [6] cause they have not been educated enough to find their way around in contemporary literature. They don't know what they may safely like in the libraries and galleries. They don't know how to judge an editorial when they see one. They don't know how to judge a political campaign. They don't know when they are being fooled by a metaphor, an analogy, a parable. And metaphor is, of course, what we are talking about. Education by poetry is education by metaphor.

Suppose we stop short of imagination, initiative, enthusiasm, inspiration, and originality—dread words. Suppose we don't mark in such things at all. There are still two minimal things, that we have got to take care of, taste and judgment. Americans are supposed to have more judgment than taste, but taste is there to be dealt with. That is what poetry, the only art in the colleges of arts, is there for. I for my part would not be afraid to go in for enthusiasm. There is the enthusiasm like a blinding light, or the enthusiasm of the deafening shout, the crude enthusiasm that you get uneducated by poetry, outside of poetry. It is ex-emplified in what I might call "sunset raving." You look westward toward the sunset, or if you get up early enough, eastward toward the sunrise, and you rave. It is oh's and ah's with you and no more.

---

[1] *Amherst Alumni Council News,* IV (March 1931), Supplement, pp. 6-13. (Reprinted from the *Amherst Graduates' Quarterly,* February 1931.)

But the enthusiasm I mean is taken through the prism of the intellect and spread on the screen in a color, all the way from hyperbole at one end—or overstatement, at one end—to understatement at the other end. It is a long strip of dark lines and and many colors. Such enthusiasm is one object of all teaching in poetry. I heard wonderful things said about Virgil yesterday, and many of them seemed to me crude enthusiasm, more like a deafening shout, many of them. But one speech had range, something of overstatement, something of statement, and something of understatement. It had all the colors of an enthusiasm passed through an idea.

I would be willing to throw away everything else but that: enthusiasm tamed by metaphor. Let me rest the case there. Enthusiasm tamed to metaphor, tamed to that much of it. I do not think anybody ever knows the discreet use of metaphor, his own and other people's, the discreet handling of metaphor, unless he has been properly educated in poetry.

Poetry begins in trivial metaphors, pretty metaphors, "grace" [7] metaphors, and goes on to the profoundest thinking that we have. Poetry provides the one permissible way of saying one thing and meaning another. People say, "Why don't you say what you mean?" We never do that, do we, being all of us too much poets. We like to talk in parables and in hints and in indirections—whether from diffidence or some other instinct.

I have wanted in late years to go further and further in making metaphor the whole of thinking. I find some one now and then to agree with me that all thinking, except mathematical thinking, is metaphorical, or all thinking except scientific thinking. The mathematical might be difficult for me to bring in, but the scientific is easy enough.

Once on a time all the Greeks were busy telling each other what the All was—or was like unto. All was three elements, air, earth, and water (we once thought it was ninety elements; now we think it is only one). All was substance, said another. All was change, said a third. But best and most fruitful was Pythagoras' comparison of the universe with number. Number of what? Number of feet, pounds, and seconds was the answer, and we had science and all that has followed in science. The metaphor has held and held, breaking down only when it came to the spiritual and psychological or the out of the way places of the physical.

The other day we had a visitor here, a noted scientist, whose latest word to the world has been that the more accurately you know where a thing is, the less accurately you are able to state how fast it is moving. You can see why that would be so, without going back to Zeno's problem of the arrow's flight. In carrying numbers into the realm of space and at the same time into the realm of time you are mixing metaphors, that is all, and you are in trouble. They won't mix. The two don't go together.

Let's take two or three more of the metaphors now in use to live by. I have just spoken of one of the new ones, a charming mixed metaphor right in the realm of higher mathematics and higher physics: that the more accurately you state where a thing is, the less accurately you will be able to tell how fast it is moving. And, of course, everything is moving. Everything is an event now. Another metaphor. A thing, they say, is an event. Do you believe it is? Not quite. I believe it is almost an event. But I like the comparison of a thing with an event. [8]

I notice another from the same quarter. "In the neighborhood of matter space is something like curved." Isn't that a good one! It seems to me that that is simply and utterly charming—to say that space is something like curved in the neighborhood of matter. "Something like."

Another amusing one is from—what is the book?—I can't say it now; but here is the metaphor. Its aim is to restore you to your ideas of free will. It wants to give you back your freedom of will. All right, here it is on a platter. You know that you can't tell by name what persons in a certain class will be dead ten years after graduation, but you can tell actuarially how many will be dead. Now, just so this scientist says of the particles of matter flying at a screen, striking a screen; you can't tell what individual particles will come, but you can say in general that a certain number will strike in a given time. It shows, you see, that the individual particle can come freely. I asked Bohr about that particularly, and he said, "Yes, it is so. It can come when it wills and as it wills; and the action of the individual particle is unpredictable. But it is not so of the action of the mass. There you can predict." He says, "That gives the individual atom its freedom, but the mass its necessity."

Another metaphor that has interested us in our time and has done all our thinking for us is the metaphor of evolution. Never mind going into the Latin word. The metaphor is simply the metaphor of the growing plant or of the growing thing. And somebody very brilliantly, quite a while ago, said that the whole universe, the whole of everything, was like unto a growing thing. That is all. I know the metaphor will break down at some point, but it has not failed everywhere. It is a very brilliant metaphor, I acknowledge, though I myself get too tired of the kind of essay that talks about the evolution of candy, we will say, or the evolution of elevators—the evolution of this, that, and the other. Everything is evolution. I emancipate myself by simply saying that I didn't get up the metaphor and so am not much interested in it.

What I am pointing out is that unless you are at home in the metaphor, unless you have had your proper poetical education in the metaphor, you are not safe anywhere. Because you are not at ease with figurative values: you don't know the metaphor in its strength and its weakness. You don't know how far you may ex- [9] pect to ride it and when it may break down with you. You are not safe in science; you are not safe in history. In history, for instance—to show that is the same in history as elsewhere—I heard somebody say yesterday that Aeneas was to be likened unto (those words, "likened unto"!) George Washington. He was that type of national hero, the middle-class man, not thinking of being a hero at all, bent on building the future, bent on his children, his descendants. A good metaphor, as far as it goes, and you must know how far. And then he added that Odysseus should be likened unto Theodore Roosevelt. I don't think that is so good. Someone visiting Gibbon at the point of death, said he was the same Gibbon as of old, still at his parallels.

Take the way we have been led into our present position morally, the world over. It is by a sort of metaphorical gradient. There is a kind of thinking—to speak metaphorically—there is a kind of thinking you might say was endemic in the brothel. It is always there. And every now and then in some mysterious way it becomes epidemic in the world. And how does it do so? By using all the good words that virtue has invented to maintain virtue. It uses honesty, first,—frankness, sincerity—those words; picks them up, uses them. "In the name of honesty, let us see what we are." You know. And then it picks up the word joy. "Let us in the name of joy, which is the enemy of our ancestors, the Puritans . . . Let us in the name of joy, which is the enemy of the kill-joy Puritan . . ." You see. "Let us," and so on. And then, "In the name of health . . ." Health is another good word. And that is the metaphor Freudianism trades on, mental health. And the first thing we know, it has us all in up to the top knot. I suppose we may blame the artists a good deal, because they are great people to spread by metaphor. The stage too—the stage is always a good intermediary between the two worlds, the under and the upper,—if I may say so without personal prejudice to the stage.

In all this I have only been saying that the devil can quote Scripture, which simply means that the good words you have lying around the devil can use for his purposes as well as anybody else. Never mind about my morality. I am not here to urge anything. I don't care whether the world is good or bad— not on any particular day.

Let me ask you to watch a metaphor breaking down here before you. [10] Somebody said to me a little while ago, "It is easy enough for me to think of the universe as a machine, as a mechanism."

I said, "You mean the universe is like a machine?"

He said, "No. I think it is one . . . Well, it is like . . ."

"I think you mean the universe is like a machine."

"All right. Let it go at that."

I asked him, "Did you ever see a machine without a pedal for the foot, or a lever for the hand, or a button for the finger?"

He said, "No—no."

I said, "All right. Is the universe like that?"

And he said, "No. I mean it is like a machine, only . . ."

" . . . it is different from a machine," I said.

He wanted to go just that far with that metaphor and no further. And so do we all. All metaphor breaks down somewhere. That is the beauty of it. It is touch and go with the metaphor, and until you have lived with it long enough you don't know when it is going. You don't know how much you can get out of it and when it will cease to yield. It is a very living thing. It is as life itself.

I have heard this ever since I can remember, and ever since I have taught: the teacher must teach the pupil to think. I saw a teacher once going around in a great school and snapping pupils' heads with thumb and finger and saying, "Think." That was when thinking was becoming the fashion. The fashion hasn't yet quite gone out.

We still ask boys in college to think, as in the nineties, but we seldom tell them what thinking means; we seldom tell them it is just putting this and that together; it is just saying one thing in terms of another. To tell them is to set their feet on the first rung of a ladder the top of which sticks through the sky.

Greatest of all attempts to say one thing in terms of another is the philosophical attempt to say matter in terms of spirit, or spirit in terms of matter, to make the final unity. That is the greatest attempt that ever failed. We stop just short there. But it is the height of poetry, the height of all thinking, the height of all poetic thinking, that attempts to say matter in terms of spirit and spirit in terms of matter. It is wrong to call anybody a materialist simply because he tries to say spirit in terms of matter, as if that were a sin. Materialism is not the attempt to say all in [11] terms of matter. The only materialist—be he poet, teacher, scientist, politician, or statesman—is the man who gets lost in his material without a gathering metaphor to throw it into shape and order. He is the lost soul.

We ask people to think, and we don't show them what thinking is. Somebody says we don't need to show them how to think; bye and bye they will think. We will give them the forms of sentences and, if they have any ideas, then they will know how to write them. But that is preposterous. All there is to writing is having ideas. To learn to write is to learn to have ideas.

The first little metaphor. . . . Take some of the trivial ones. I would rather have trivial ones of my own to live by than the big ones of other people.

I remember a boy saying, "He is the kind of person that wounds with his shield." That may be a slender one, of course. It goes a good way in character description. It has poetic grace. "He is the kind that wounds with his shield."

The shield reminds me—just to linger a minute—the shield reminds me of the inverted shield spoken of in one of the books of the *Odyssey*, the book that tells about the longest swim on record. I forget how long it lasted—several days, was it?—but at last Odysseus came near the coast of Phoenicia, he saw it on the horizon "like an inverted shield."

There is a better metaphor in the same book. In the end Odysseus comes ashore and crawls up the beach to spend the night under a double olive tree, and it says, as in a lonely farmhouse where it is hard to get fire—I am not quoting exactly —where it is hard to start the fire again if it goes out, they cover the seeds of fire with ashes to preserve it for the night, so Odysseus covered himself with the leaves around him and went to sleep. There you have something that gives you character, something of Odysseus himself. "Seeds of fire." So Odysseus covered the seeds of fire in himself. You get the greatness of his nature.

But these are slighter metaphors than the ones we live by. They have their charm, their passing charm. They are as it were the first steps toward the great thoughts, grave thoughts, thoughts lasting to the end.

The metaphor whose manage we are best taught in poetry— that is all there is of thinking. It may not seem far for the mind [12] to go but it is the mind's furthest. The richest accumulation of the ages is the noble metaphors we have rolled up.

I want to add one thing more that the experience of poetry is to anyone who comes close to poetry. There are two ways of coming close to poetry. One is by writing poetry. And some people think I want people to write poetry, but I don't; that is, I don't necessarily. I only want people to write poetry if they want to write poetry. I have never encouraged anybody to write poetry that did not want to write it, and I have not always encouraged those who did want to write it. That ought to be one's own funeral. It is a hard, hard life, as they say.

(I have just been to a city in the West, a city full of poets, a city they have made safe for poets. The whole city is so lovely that you do not have to write it up to make it poetry; it is ready-made for you. But, I don't know—the poetry written in that city might not seem like poetry if read outside of the city. It would be like the jokes made when you were drunk; you have to get drunk again to appreciate them.)

But as I say, there is another way to come close to poetry, fortunately, and that is in the reading of it, not as linguistics, not as history, not as anything but poetry. It is one of the hard things for a teacher to know how close a man has come in reading poetry. How do I know whether a man has come close to Keats in reading Keats? It is hard for me to know. I have lived with some boys a whole year over some of the poets and I have not felt sure whether they have come near what it was all about. One remark sometimes told me. One remark was their mark for the year; had to be—it was all I got that told me what I wanted to know. And that is enough, if it was the right remark, if it came close enough. I think a man might make twenty fool remarks if he made one good one some time in the year. His mark would depend on that good remark.

The closeness—everything depends on the closeness with which you come, and you ought to be marked for the closeness, for nothing else. And that will have to be estimated by chance remarks, not by question and answer. It is only by accident that you know some day how near a person has come. [13]

⚘ "THE CONSTANT SYMBOL" [2]

There seems to be some such folk saying as that easy to understand is contemptible, hard to understand irritating. The implication is that just easy enough, just hard enough, right in the middle, is what literary criticism ought to foster. A glance backward over the past convinces me otherwise. The *Iliad*, *Odyssey*, and *Aeneid* are easy. The *Purgatorio* is said to be hard. The Song of Songs *is* hard. There have been works lately to surpass all records for hardness. Some knotted riddles tell that may be worth our trouble. But hard or easy seems to me of slight use as a test either way.

Texture is surely something. A good piece of weaving takes rank with a picture as decoration for the wall of a studio, though it must be admitted to verge on the arty. There is a time of apprenticeship to texture when it shouldn't matter if the stuff is never made up into anything. There may be scraps of repeated form all over it. But form as a whole! Don't be shocking! The title of his first book was *Fragments*. The artist has to grow

---

[2] *Atlantic Monthly*, CLXXVIII (October 1946), 50-52.

up and coarsen a little before he looks on texture as not an end in itself.

And there are many other things I have found myself saying about poetry, but the chiefest of these is that it is metaphor, saying one thing and meaning another, saying one thing in terms of another, the pleasure of ulteriority. Poetry is simply made of metaphor. So also is philosophy—and science, too, for that matter, if it will take the soft impeachment from a friend. Every poem is a new metaphor inside or it is nothing. And there is a sense in which all poems are the same old metaphor always.

Every single poem written regular is a symbol small or great of the way the will has to pitch into commitments deeper and deeper to a rounded conclusion and then be judged for whether any original intention it had has been strongly spent or weakly lost; be it in art, politics, school, church, business, love, or marriage—in a piece of work or in a career. Strongly spent is synonymous with kept.

We may speak after sentence, resenting judgment. How can the world know anything so intimate as what we were intending to do? The answer is the world presumes to know. The ruling passion in man is not as Viennese as is claimed. It is rather a gregarious instinct to keep together by minding each other's business. Grex rather than sex. We *must* be preserved from becoming egregious. The beauty of socialism is that it will end the individuality that is always crying out mind your own business. Terence's answer would be all human business is my business. No more invisible means of support, no more invisible motives, no more invisible anything. The ultimate commitment is giving in to it that an outsider may see what we were up to sooner and better than we ourselves. The bard has said in effect, Unto these forms did I commend the spirit. It may take him a year after the act to confess he only betrayed the spirit with a rhymster's cleverness and to forgive his enemies the critics for not having listened to his oaths and protestations to the contrary. Had he anything to be true to? Was he true to it? Did he use good words? You couldn't tell unless you made out what idea they were supposed to be good for. Every poem is an epitome of the great predicament; a figure of the will braving alien entanglements.

Take the President in the White House. A study of the success of his intention might have to go clear back to when as a young politician, youthfully step-careless, he made choice between the two parties of our system. He may have stood for a moment wishing he knew of a third party nearer the ideal; but only for a moment, since he was practical. And in fact he may have been so little impressed with the importance of his choice that he left his first commitment to be made for him by his friends and relatives. It was only a small commitment anyway, like a kiss. He can scarcely remember how much credit he deserved personally for the decision it took. Calculation is usually no part in the first step in any walk. And behold him now a statesman so multifariously closed in on with obligations and answerabilities that sometimes he loses his august temper. He might as well have got himself into a sestina royal.

Or he may be a religious nature who lightly gets committed to a nameable church through an older friend in plays and games at the Y.M.C.A. The [50] next he knows he is in a theological school and next in the pulpit of a Sunday wrestling with the angel for a blessing on his self-defensive interpretation of the Creed. What of his original intention now? At least he has had the advantage of having it more in his heart than in his head; so that he should have made shift to assert it without being chargeable with compromise. He could go a long way before he had to declare anything he could be held to. He began with freedom to squander. He has to acknowledge himself in a tighter and tighter place. But his courage asked for it. It would have been the same if he had gone to the North Pole or climbed Everest. All that concerns *us* is whether his story was one of conformance or performance.

There's an indulgent smile I get for the recklessness of the unnecessary commitment I made when I came to the first line in the second stanza of a poem in my book called "Stopping by Woods on a Snowy Evening." I was riding too high to care what trouble I incurred. And it was all right so long as I didn't suffer deflection.

The poet goes in like a rope skipper to make the most of his opportunities. If he trips himself, he stops the rope. He is of our stock and has been brought up by ear to choice of two metres, strict iambic and loose iambic (not to count varieties of the latter). He may have any length of line up to six feet. He may use an assortment of line lengths for any shape of stanza, like Herrick in "To Daffodils." Not that he is running wild. His intention is of course a particular mood that won't be satisfied with anything less than its own fulfillment. But it is not yet a thought concerned with what becomes it. One thing to know it by: it shrinks shyly from anticipatory expression. Tell love beforehand and, as Blake says, it loses flow without filling the mould; the cast will be a reject. The freshness of a poem belongs absolutely to its not having been thought out and then set to verse as the verse in turn might be set to music. A poem is the emotion of having a thought while the reader waits a little anxiously for the success of dawn. The only discipline to begin with is the inner mood that at worst may give the poet a false start or two like the almost microscopic filament of cotton that goes before the blunt thread-end and must be picked up first by the eye of the needle. He must be entranced to the exact premonition. No mystery is meant. When familiar friends approach each other in the street both are apt to have this experience in feeling before knowing the pleasantry they will inflict on each other in passing.

Probably there is something between the mood and the vocal imagination (images of the voice speaking) that determines a man's first commitment to metre and length of line.

Suppose him to have written down "When in disgrace with Fortune and men's eyes." He has uttered about as much he has to live up to in the theme as in the form. Odd how the two advance into the open *pari passu*. He has given out that he will descend into Hades, but he has confided in no one how far before he will turn back, or whether he will turn back at all, and by what jutting points of rock he will pick his way. He may proceed as in blank verse. Two lines more, however, and he has let himself in for rhyme, three more and he has set himself a stanza. Up to this point his discipline has been the self-discipline whereof it is written in so great praise. The harsher discipline from without is now well begun. He who knows not both knows neither. His worldly commitments are now three or four deep. Between us, he was no doubt bent on the sonnet in the first place from habit, and what's the use in pretending he was a freer agent than he had any ambition to be. He had made most of his commitments all in one plunge. The only suspense he asks us to share with him is in the theme. He goes down, for instance, to a depth that must surprise him as much as it does us. But he doesn't even have the say of how long his piece will be. Any worry is as to whether he will outlast or last out the fourteen lines—have to cramp or stretch to come out even—have enough bread for the butter or butter for the bread. As a matter of fact, he gets through in twelve lines and doesn't know quite what to do with the last two.

Things like that and worse are the reason the sonnet is so suspect a form and has driven so many to free verse and even to the novel. Many a quatrain is salvaged from a sonnet that went agley. Dobson confesses frankly to having changed from one form to another after starting: "I intended an Ode, And it turned to a Sonnet." But he reverses the usual order of being driven from the harder down to the easier. And he has a better excuse for weakness of will than most, namely, Rose.

Jeremiah, it seems, has had his sincerity questioned because the anguish of his lamentations was tamable to the form of twenty-two stanzas for the twenty-two letters of the alphabet. The Hebrew alphabet has been kept to the twenty-two letters it came out of Egypt with, so the number twenty-two means as much form as ever.

But there they go again with the old doubt about law and order. (The communist looks forward to a day of order without law, bless his merciful heart.) To the right person it must seem naïve to distrust form as such. The very words of the dictionary are a restriction to make the best of or stay out of and be silent. Coining new words isn't encouraged. We play the words as we find them. We make them do. Form in language is such a disjected lot of old broken pieces it seems almost as non-existent as the spirit till the two embrace in the sky. They are not to be thought of as encountering in rivalry but in creation. No judgment on either alone counts. We see what Whitman's extravagance may have meant when he said the body was the soul. [51]

Here is where it all comes out. The mind is a baby giant who, more provident in the cradle than he knows, has hurled his paths in life all round ahead of him like playthings given—data so-called. They are vocabulary, grammar, prosody, and diary, and it will be too bad if he can't find stepping stones of them for his feet wherever he wants to go. The way will be zigzag, but it will be a straight crookedness like the walking stick he cuts himself in the bushes for an emblem. He will be judged as he does or doesn't let this zig or that zag project him off out of his general direction.

Teacher or student or investigator whose chance on these defenseless lines may seize, your pardon if for once I point you out what ordinarily you would point me out. To some it will seem strange that I should have written my verse regular all this time without knowing till yesterday that it was from fascination with this constant symbol I celebrate. To the right person it will seem lucky; since in finding out too much too soon there is danger of arrest. Does anyone believe I would have committed myself to the treason-reason-season rhyme-set in my "Reluctance" if I had been blasé enough to know that these three words about exhausted the possibilities? No rhyming dictionary for me to make me face the facts of rhyme. I may say the strain of rhyming is less since I came to see words as phrase-ends to countless phrases just as the syllables *ly*, *ing*, and *ation* are word-ends to countless words. Leave something to learn still later. We'd have lost most of our innocence by forty anyway even if we never went to school a day.

TO THE RIGHT PERSON

Fourteen Lines

In the one state of ours that is a shire
There is a District Schoolhouse I admire—
As much as anything for situation.
There are few institutions standing higher
This side the Rockies in my estimation—
Two thousand feet above the ocean level.
It has two entries for co-education.
But there's a tight-shut look to either door
And to the windows of its fenestration
As if to say mere knowledge was the devil,
And this school wasn't keeping any more,
Unless for penitents who took their seat
Upon its doorsteps as at Mercy's feet
To make up for a lack of meditation. [52]

❧ GENERAL CRITICISM

❧ ELIZABETH SHEPLEY SERGEANT[1]

Robert Frost's spirit is native to all high, sweet-smelling, lonely slopes which command, as from a remove, the homes and the graves of men. Of such places he has seemed to me, ever since I first read *A Boy's Will*, the *genius loci*. If I watched long enough, he might put off his trick of invisibility and show his head above a blueberry bush or a boulder. No doubt I have searched for him most persistently in the pastures below the ledgy shoulder of Chocorua, but I once thought I spied him in a sunburned cliff city of New Mexico, and his elusive figure is associated with the high glare of Delphi, and with those jagged little peaks of southern France whence the scent of herbs rises like incense. Those who mistake his verse for a product local or provincial have been too literal. They have failed to catch the poet in his game of hide-and-seek. Frost does hide, if he can, in [285] verse or out. The language of his poetry, though so markedly that of New England speech, is symbolic; his subject-matter, for all its clear geographical limits, is universal. Through the realism of the lines, stars and "charted meteors" are always piercing. Like his friend the Star-Splitter, Frost seems once for all to have burned down his house for the insurance, and spent the proceeds on a telescope,

> To satisfy a life-long curiosity
> About our place among the infinities.

He has been interrogating the heavens ever since. That may be the reason why he is still, as he puts it in "New Hampshire"— the most openly autobiographical of his poems—"a rascal," instead of the learned doctor or the celebrated bard he might be if he chose.

---

[1] From "Robert Frost: Good Greek out of New England," *Fire Under the Andes*, New York: Knopf, 1927, pp. 285-294. Copyright 1927, 1955 by, and reprinted by permission of, the author.

A kind of professor he has had to be in spite of himself, since most good Greeks—Frost almost admits himself one in "New Hampshire," as well as a plain farmer—from Socrates on have needed to add youth to their star-gazing. Frost affirms that he has "never earned a cent, save from and through verse. But for my first twenty years at it I earned a total of two hundred dollars." Farming and teaching, those two subsidiary occupations with which he has had almost as lifelong a connection as with the infinities, grew somehow out [286] of his poems, as poems so surely grew out of them. In the early days it was more farming than teaching. Latterly it has been the other way about. Frost is too suspicious of formal learning to have become a pedagogue easily. It was not, so he tells, until he found the store-keeper at Derry, New Hampshire—where by the grace of a grandfather with no faith in the Muses he had that first farm of his—appraising his horse for the grocery bill that he decided to apply (with a poem) at Pinkerton Academy. He would prove to the world of men that he could have as much practical success as he wanted. But there was more for Frost in teaching than a solution of household economics, or we should not find him still trailing, in the Amherst hills or the Michigan flats, his troop of college boys.

Even when he consents to sit on a platform he has a vanishing and peripatetic look, and the doctrine he enunciates in his dry, sly, halting way is very different from the glib æstheticism his students might expect of a poet. Perfectionist and polisher of words though he is, he proclaims words to be "less than nothing unless they amount to deeds, as in ultimatums and battle cries." In poetry, as in life, there is no worth in being unless it is allied to doing. And what kind of professor is this who gives you no synthetic appreciations, and forces you to speculate? The day I saw [287] him on an Amherst platform he was steering his class towards the reading of Emerson by asking it to define an "idealist." Is he a man who measures up from nothing, or one who measures down from everything? Might he be, especially if an artist, somewhere between the two? "I believe in what the Greeks called synecdoche: the philosophy of the part for the whole; skirting the hem of the goddess. All that an artist needs is samples. Enough success to know what money is like; enough love to know what women are like." Enough time, he might have added, for creative puttering; enough thin books of verse to fill half a foot of shelf. Frost is always bedevilling his students with questions, but never with one—this is his cardinal principle as an educator—which he can answer himself. For example this poser: How many things can you do to a poem besides read it or write it? The class found one hundred and eight. Compare the passage in "A Fountain":

> How had the tender verse escaped their outrage?
> By being invisible for what it was,
> Or else by some remoteness that defied them
> To find out what to do to hurt a poem.

One of the outstanding facts about Robert Frost is that he and his verse were buried for twenty years in the rocky quietude of New Hampshire. It is not so sure that even now college students —[288] or for that matter college teachers, publishers, editors, critics, and friendly readers—know what to make of the cast of mind and spirit of a good Greek disguised as a Yankee sage.

The cast of feature bears out the cast of mind. If I could choose a sculptor from the antique world to mould Frost's head, I should vote for Scopas, who added shadows of human passion to calm Greek faces. In certain moods, this Frost face with its musing eyes, so deeply hollowed and shaded by sharp-drawn brows, seems touched by that pathetic hand. But again the poet's dream grows unified, grave, mystical-religious, and one says, Here are a brow and eyes like Dante's. At the dinner in honour of Frost's fiftieth birthday at the Hotel Brevoort, in New York, he wore at first this marble Dantesque mask; coloured really like Carrara marble, with mauve and golden shadows, and shining with a clear Renaissance beauty of the Christian sort. Frost should have wrapped himself in a white Dominican gown to celebrate his half century. For he carried almost visibly the consecration and weight of his ascetic priesthood.

Yet it took only a featherweight of affection—all that the friends dared offer, since they had come, for the most part, with the hands that bore gifts tied behind their backs—to make tenderness flicker like flame over the still features, and shape [289] itself in facial line; only a quip of New England humour to bring a gentle cynic out of hiding. Or shall I say a rustic deity? Eyebrows arch roundly, cheeks draw into shrewd, satiric wrinkles, eyes turn to flashes and darts of blue light, malicious or rejoicing, and as an unruly lock is tossed, one hears the stamp of a hoof—

> Pan came out of the woods one day,—
> His skin and his hair and his eyes were grey . . .

Frost's skin and his rebellious hair have now a fine harmony of tone, "the grey of the moss of walls," a young and living greyness that, like a delicate lichen, softens without hiding the hard and eternal shape of the rock beneath.

> —a new-world song, far out of reach.

that is what the rascally Pan of the haunting Yankee pipe came out of the woods to play. Poetry has not flowed in a swelling stream from the pipe of Robert Frost; it has been distilled within him preciously, like heart's-blood, drop by drop. The verse reveals a keen warfare between the Puritan who thought shame of revelation, and the artist who had to speak out, a battle never wholly won or lost, yet probably serving him well. For the inhibitions and reticences of the Dantesque or Puritan Frost have imposed on the sensuous singing Frost that austere and elegant poetical outline of [290] his. It is not as enigmatic as it seems to some of the young intellectuals that he should have preferred frugality to luxury in many realms of culture, knowledge, and experience. His anti-æsthetic prejudices, for instance, are essential to him. He does not want superlatives. A rather bare world suits him. His doubt of the trappings and self-indulgences of the artist, which has in it more of judgment than he usually allows himself (think how little there is in his New England narratives), is a sort of armour to preserve his poetry intact. He will not talk of art in his poetry except in symbolic terms, as in "The Axe-Helve," where he endows a French workman with desires and aims he can scarcely admit. And how deliberately he makes his artistic ego the butt of his malice:

> I'm what is called a sensibilitist,
> Or otherwise an environmentalist. . . .
> In other words, I know wherever I am,
> Being the creature of literature I am,
> I shall not lack for pains to keep me awake.

("Not so you'd notice it," appends a Frostian note in pencil, "but still too much so for self-approval." *Self-approval*—there the

Puritan shows his spots. The sensibility is, however, allowed.)

The satiric wrinkle that lifts the corner of his long upper lip tells the whole story. In the heart of his starkest tragedy we find the old New England [291] effort to compromise ideals and facts, escaping either in shy tenderness and beauty or in a whimsical humour that often verges on irony. Consider for tenderness "An Old Man's Winter Night"—one of Frost's ultimates in the union of form and substance; for humour "A Hundred Collars," and you will see that what looks like fancy is no more nor less than a fact. Yes, there is something strong and steady in Frost's spirit which takes account of his compromises, and holds the twisted strands of his life together for one central purpose. The claim one makes for him of first-rateness—he will make few claims for himself—rests in part on his sureness and continuity of poetic development. In life he has turned from one task to another, but in verse he has stuck with piety to the clarification of his own tone of voice, his own form and matter. If he is "Greek" it is not that he is truly pagan, but only that he has known how to choose from the world exactly what he needed for himself and his song—for himself as a singer.

One of the things he needed and found was a normal human destiny. Born in San Francisco; brought up from the age of ten by a mother and a grandfather in Lawrence, Massachusetts; looking in—no more—at Dartmouth College; he married young a very true New England girl—a marriage preserved like treasure through the years—retired [292] to his rustic isolation of farming and teaching, and had in time four children, now launched in their own life paths. In all these level solitary seasons Frost was writing poetry with solid faith in his mission, though editors seemed to make little of it. When he stole away with his family on his decisive voyage to England in 1912, at the age of thirty-eight, the world where reputations are made was none the wiser, and he himself was far from conceiving that triumphant return two years later after the English publication of *A Boy's Will* and *North of Boston*. Yet here were the editors drawn up on the dock, hailing him as a leader of his generation in the "new poetry"; here were rewards and successes which made farming somewhat vicarious and gave teaching a privileged academic form; here was leisure to produce *Mountain Interval* and *New Hampshire*. These books reveal that neither the "new poetry" nor the new opportunity have taken Frost farther from his native base than the stride to Michigan. You can find just one English poem—if you look hard: "The Sound of the Trees." Frost recognized early that, like his Census-Taker, he wanted life to go on living; but he has sought it where he stood.

The life he found, as revealed in his books, has a pattern, a colour, above all a sound, that must vanish like mist in the prose telling. Its background is a landscape, pearly in tone, lonely to [293] those who do not recognize its friendliness; northern New England, broken in outline, with views but not giant views, mountains but not too high ones, pastures, swamps, farms deserted and farms occupied. This land, to the spare human figures who move across it, is an extension and explanation of themselves, as the Irish country to the fairy folk. And these New Englanders are somehow "folk" in addition to being real people and even local "characters." They are planted here by necessity, their roots are tangled in the roots of elm and cedar, their wisdom is all garnered from natural things. Those who find Frost's poetry sad and grey probably cannot bear the sheer clarity he gives to human lives in this thin northern atmosphere of his, shut in by a moral and physical solitude, yet escaping through their barriers to grapple together in situations of love and hate and suffering typical and inevitable of New England but also of "the world in general." [294]

❧ J. MC BRIDE DABBS[2]

. . . there is one image which, both by its character and by the frequency of its appearance, suggests that it has a special personal value. This is the image of a wood.

As we consider this image, it will appear that, with few exceptions, the wood, for Frost, symbolizes nature itself with its challenge and its fascination:

> . . . your woods . . .
> Waiting to steal a step on us whenever
> We drop our eyes or turn to other things. . . .

[2] From "Robert Frost and the Dark Woods," *Yale Review*, **XXIII** (Spring 1934), 514-520. Reprinted by permission of *The Yale Review*. Copyright by Yale University Press.

The mountain pushed us off her knees,
And now her lap is full of trees.

The wood as an object of fascination recurs many times. "Into My Own," the first poem of *A Boy's Will* (evidently [517] considered important by Frost because he included it as the last in the *Selected Poems*), is significant here. The poet wishes that "those dark trees" stretched away to the edge of doom. If they did—

> I should not be withheld but that some day
> Into their vastness I should steal away,
> Fearless of ever finding open land,
> Or highway where the slow wheel pours the sand.

But he is already realizing the danger of this withdrawal. One may go too far—into oneself?—to be found:

> So all who hide too well away
> Must speak and tell us where they are.

He is realizing also the danger to his art.

In "The Sound of the Trees," which is the (later) summer counterpart of "Now Close the Windows," and in which the attraction of the silently tossing winter trees of the earlier poem is deepened by the sound of summer leaves, the poet wonders why we wish to suffer this endless noise of trees about us. Is it not because they speak to us of going?—arouse in us the old natural desire to wander, and call us away from the fixed joys and measured pace of social life into vague distances and leafy depths?

> I shall set forth for somewhere,
> I shall make the reckless choice
> Some day when they are in voice
> And tossing so as to scare
> The white clouds over them on.
> I shall have less to say.
> But I shall be gone.

It is hard to say whether this fascination for Frost of woods and trees ever becomes a distinct fear of them or not. He represents such a fear in "The Oft-Repeated Dream." He expresses it

98

again in "New Hampshire," in the reference to the man suffering from dendrophobia, who [518]

> . . . Knew too well for any earthly use
> The line where man leaves off and nature starts,
> And never over-stepped it save in dreams.

Afraid or not, the fascination is evident. And it gives to the somewhat classic poetry of Robert Frost a distinct romantic quality. He glances longingly at lonely woods, hesitates, and looks back towards men.

It is this hesitancy, charming in Frost, that makes him so modern. He is forever steering straight off into space. His lonely flight into the unknown, into distance, into the future, his spirit of discovery, is ours. Ours, too, is the weakening will that limits the flight. We are not sure, now, that we long for the unknown and lonely; we pause and look back. To the romantic twilight of secluded places, we have added the modern twilight of doubt whether we should venture farther, or relinquish the quest and come home.

Frost's most perfect lyric perhaps, "Stopping by Woods on a Snowy Evening," is the final expression of this modern temper. On first reading I valued it for its excellent fusion of freshness and richness, its complete and accurate picture of the humorous shy poet, the pony giving his harness bells a shake, and "The darkest evening of the year." Now I value it for this, and for something else. For the portrait of Robert Frost himself, with those inimitable last lines:

> The woods are lovely, dark and deep,
> But I have promises to keep,
> And miles to go before I sleep,
> And miles to go before I sleep.

Though the thought still pushes forward, wood-magic has made of the words an incantation to sleep.

And I value this lyric for its picture of life. I know of no other symbol in Frost's poetry that, partly because of the appropriate music, says so much as this. Here at least [519] the "clear and classical" Frost has adopted something of the technique of Symbolism, that vague shadow of Romanticism. "To approximate the indefiniteness of music," says Edmund Wilson, was "one of the principal aims of Symbolism." In "Stopping by Woods on a Snowy Evening" we hear the more than human music of a typical human situation, the insistent whisper of death at the heart of life. For we are all travellers, travelling alone through haunted country. Strange voices lure us away to nature, friendly voices call us back to men. Whichever call we heed, we sleep at last. And often to-day, in tragic indecision, confused by the conflicting voices, we fall asleep murmuring of the miles we have to go. [520]

ẅ GRANVILLE HICKS[3]

Robert Frost also has a world of his own, and his great advantage over [Edwin Arlington] Robinson lies in the fact that his world is, to some extent, identified with a particular area as it has existed at a particular time. Though his world is as compact and as nearly self-sufficient as the less tangible realm over which Robinson rules, any one who has traveled north of Boston can recognize the language he speaks, the scenery he describes, and the people he presents. Yet it cannot be denied that Frost has achieved unity by a definite process of exclusion. One not only realizes that life in New Hampshire is not altogether representative of life in the United States as a whole; one has to admit that Frost disregards many elements in New Hampshire life, and especially the elements that link that state with the rest of the country. For example, northern New England has been greatly affected by the growth of industrialism, and yet one would never suspect this from Frost's poetry. Can one believe that it is by accident that he has never written of the factory towns, now so abjectly in decay, or of the exodus to the cities and its failure, now so apparent, to bring deliverance? Has he never heard of the [245] railroads and their influence on the state's politics, touching the smallest hamlet? Do not automobiles and radios exist in New Hampshire? No, Frost is too shrewd not to be well aware that he is excluding from his poems whatever might destroy their unity. He knows the full value of his self-imposed limitations,

[3] From *The Great Tradition*, New York: Macmillan, 1935, pp. 245-246.

and he is even willing to boast of his good fortune in the parable
of the star in the stone boat:

> Such as it is, it promises the prize
> Of the one world complete in any size
> That I am like to compass, fool or wise.

Much of Frost's experience is close to ours, and we can share
his appreciations and his insights. His strong narratives, his clear
and unpretentious lyrics, and his thoughtful, sensible allegories
are more satisfying than most poetry of our day. But, to the
extent that his imagination concerns itself only with what is
personally congenial and poetically available, he too leaves us
discontented. For all his common sense and his originality, he
has chosen to identify himself with a moribund tradition. Many
poets, these hundred and fifty years, have written of mountains,
fields, and brooks, and of farmers at their humble tasks; these
things have become part of our imaginative inheritance, and one
must be insensitive indeed not to be conscious of the beauty in
them. But there are other objects now more frequently before
our eyes—factories, skyscrapers, machines. We see mechanics,
shopgirls, truck-drivers, more often than we do farmers, and we
see the farmer not as a romantic figure but as the victim of cruel
economic forces. There is new territory that we beg the poet
to conquer for us. Perhaps to-day no poet is capable of that
conquest, but, if the task is ever to be accomplished, some one
with the talent of a Robert Frost must make a beginning. [246]

❦ PAUL ENGLE[4]

When I was a boy in the Middle West of America, in that
rich prairie farming land where rivers as long and broad as the
Mississippi and Missouri seem lost, a friend gave me a book of
poems by Robert Frost. He had been a farmer in his youth, and
his hands that gave me the book were still the square-fingered
and coarse-lined hands that had swung the scythe and gripped the
plough. "It's the real thing," he said, "and no fooling. He knows
what he's talking about."

---

[4] "Preface" to Frost's *Selected Poems*, London: Cape, 1936, pp. 23-28.

Robert Frost, I found, did know what he was talking about. The man who wrote this was familiar with springs; he had pulled out of them the leaves of oak and maple and watched the water bubble the mud away till it was clear as air:

> I'm going out to clean the pasture spring;
> I'll only stop to rake the leaves away
> (And wait to watch the water clear, I may):
> I sha'n't be gone long.—You come too.

But there was something more than the eye that had seen the simple thing, and written of it with an equal [23] simplicity. All the things were true, the broken walls, the wood pile that warmed "the frozen swamp as best it could With the slow smokeless burning of decay," the white-tailed bird whose suspicion was that of "one who takes Everything said as personal to himself." But there was something else. It was the sense of a land that was not the countryside where I had watched wood piles rot and followed birds over hills. It wasn't just that the feeling in these lines,

> It doesn't seem so much to climb a mountain
> You've worked around the foot of all your life,

was strange because the nearest mountain was a thousand miles away. Nor was it alone the oxen in the lines:

> And there I met a man who moved so slow
> With white-faced oxen in a heavy cart,
> It seemed no harm to stop him altogether.

We had no oxen in Iowa, the farmers thundered into town in two-ton trucks, and though they might stop if you were hitch-hiking and thumbed them for a ride, they'd consider the stop as time lost and try to make it up. But it wasn't the difference between trucks and oxen. It was one mind against another mind. One integrated part of America against another part.

The regions of the United States stretch out like the points of a compass from a central point, like Kansas City, or some little sand town in western Nebraska. I had known a few, the Southwest where the Spaniards [24] left blooded horses and wild Indian children and names like the Blood of Christ mountains. The deep South where the way of cooking a chicken is a matter of family pride, and crippled negroes wander the roads under the live-oaks. But north of Boston I had never been. And here was that area in a book. It was a place where men had lived for what was, in America, a long time on the same length of earth. It was a group of states whose names, to one who was young, in a young state, were not so much real places as the call words of history. The people in it were old enough to know their neighbour so well as to suspect him. Out West we still used the word "neighbour" as equivalent to "friend," because in our minds we remembered the frontier, when a neighbour was valuable, a lender of tools and work and a little coffee. Those New Englanders had been there long enough to build granite defences for themselves—where else in America could the man who lived next door to you have as a saying, "Good fences make good neighbours"? They had lived on the same land till the life was sucked out of it and the plough harvested only rocks, and the barns had wooden cages in the darkest corners where the minds that had cracked under in-breeding and the lonely, repressive life in remote valleys, under the weight of a morality like November mist defying the sun by day and the lantern by night, gibbered their life away.

All these Robert Frost had seen and remembered. His verse was a slow plough, turning them up, bringing [25] the undersoil to light. He knew the temper of men who could say to their wife, with the coffin of their dead child in the parlour waiting to be buried,

> Three foggy mornings and one rainy day
> Will rot the best birch fence a man can build.

But he knew that they couldn't draw back all the time, that sooner or later they would have to face the approach of other men, and

> Doors locked and curtains drawn will make no difference.

It was more than a region of America that I learned from Robert Frost. There was as much in the way he said things, as in the things themselves. Reading his poems, it seemed that a man speaking in a measured way was as close as one could come to defining poetry. Whether in direct speech or in simple description, Frost's poetry was like a man speaking. It was an easy, swinging, cadenced line, responsive more to the movement of voice than of metre. There is a similar rhythm in:

> Part of a moon was falling down the west,
> Dragging the whole sky with it to the hills.

And in:

> Of course he's nothing to us, any more
> Than was the hound that came a stranger to us
> Out of the woods, worn out upon the trail. [26]

In any kind of verse, even lyrical, there is this careful casualness:

> But I am done with apple-picking now.
> Essence of winter sleep is on the night,
> The scent of apples: I am drowsing off.
> I cannot rub the strangeness from my sight
> I got from looking through a pane of glass
> I skimmed this morning from the drinking trough.

It is this conviction that the words were actually spoken—are being spoken by the reader as he sees them—that confirms the mood of truthfulness in all Frost's verse. True things—in the sense of actual things that have not been changed, but only heightened by the imagination—are said in a true way, whether they are chicken-carrying:

> We're not allowed to take them upside down,
> Two at a time's the rule, one on each arm . . .
> We fence our flowers in and the hens range,

or a man and a woman in sorrow. He speaks:

> Don't carry it to someone else this time.
> Tell me about it if it's something human.
> Let me into your grief. I'm not so much
> Unlike other folks as your standing there
> Apart would make me out.

Yet it is not alone the voice of New England, whether talking about apple-picking in a book of poems or in [27] New Hampshire orchards. It is also the mood of speech that is in vast sections of America, the easy, loose way of saying everything that sustains equally American humour and American poetry. It is part of the native genius of Robert Frost that he has caught this colloquial rhythm, and realized that, because it is both an honest and an expressive way of saying things, it is the surest medium for an American who wants to talk simply and strongly. That was the way Will Rogers talked in his cowboy jokes. That is also the way Robert Frost talks in poem after poem. He knows that "all the fun's in how you say a thing." [28]

Ẃ CLEANTH BROOKS[5]

Robert Frost is a regionalist and a traditionalist. Yet his poetry differs sharply from that of the poets discussed in the previous chapters. And in the popular mind it differs more sharply still. He is popularly supposed to be homely, salty, direct, whereas poets like Ransom and Tate are reputed to be tortured intellectual obscurantists. The presumption is that the structure of his poetry differs radically from the structure of theirs.

A thoughtful reading will show that Frost's poetry, however salty and homely, is scarcely direct. The casual reader may receive an impression of directness because Frost works so constantly in terms of anecdote, incident, and character sketch—elements which have no special associations with the pure technique of poetry. But the *poetry* of Frost does not inhere in these elements; on the contrary, he employs these elements as means to the end of poetry. The reader, then, should ask himself how they are related to the central method, and should not consider them as ends in themselves. (In fairness to the reader, it ought to be said that Frost has encouraged this misapprehension by his frequent laxity in building his elements into a form.)

Frost's anecdotes, incidents, character sketches do have a surface directness; but, as poet, he employs them for purposes of indirection. What sets him off from the poets already discussed is not, for example, a lack of irony, but, first, the context in which the irony appears, and second, [110] the level at which it operates. Characteristically, it appears at the level of licensed whimsy, or of dry understatement.

---

[5] From *Modern Poetry and the Tradition*, Chapel Hill: University of North Carolina, 1939, pp. 110-114.

The whimsy is licensed by being made a mannerism of the New England character. That character (it does not concern the present issue whether it is Frost's own character or merely a mask which he adopts as poet) may be described as follows: the sensitive New Englander, possessed of a natural wisdom; dry and laconic when serious; genial and whimsical when not; a character who is uneasy with hyperbole and prefers to use understatement to risking possible overstatement.

The range of Frost's poetry is pretty thoroughly delimited by the potentialities for experience possessed by such a character. The poetry will rarely lapse into sentimentality. It will not allow itself to become grandiose. But on the other hand, because of its fear of overreaching itself, it will rarely aspire to any great intensity. The virtues of Frost's poetry, in short, are solid ones—virtues produced by a strong sense of dramatic decorum.

Much of Frost's poetry hardly rises above the level of the vignette of rural New England. Consider the genre piece, "The Code." The incident related occurs in the New England haying season. The theme is that the New England yeoman has his code of honor too: he will not be "told" to hurry or take pains. But the ironic tension is pretty well limited to the title itself. Except for the idiomatic and flexible blank verse, Frost makes use of no resources in the poem not available to the accomplished short story writer. The poetry is diluted and diffuse. A significant symptom of the diffuseness is the absence of metaphor. The very minimum of imagery is used.

In general, Frost's metaphors are few and tame; and the occasional bold metaphor is confined to his very lightest poems: for example, to such a sally of self-ironic whimsy as "Canis Major." Frost does not think through his images; he requires statements. The audacity of his metaphor is thus in inverse proportion to the seriousness of the experience. [111]

This same basic timidity often prevents the anecdotes from developing into fables or symbols. Frost's themes are frequently stated overtly, outside the symbolical method; the poet comes downstage to philosophize explicitly.

Thus, in "Two Tramps in Mud Time," the point of the poem is explicitly stated in the last stanza:

> My object in living is to unite
> My avocation and my vocation. . . .

> Only where love and need are one,
> And the work is play for mortal stakes,
> Is the deed ever really done. . . .

The statement, of course, is given a *raison d'être* in terms of an incident. The speaker is chopping wood and having a great deal of pleasure in his activity when two tramps from the lumber-camps come by and pause to ask for the job. He enjoys the work, but he realizes that he has no moral right to deprive the men of a job which they need.

The first stanza sketches in the situation. The poet does not hurry on to moralize on it. He toys with what is to be his decision while he goes on to chatter about the changeableness of the northern spring, the satisfaction of making the beech blocks fall

> . . . splinterless as a cloven rock

and the pleasure of the physical exercise. There is the mildly ironic self-depreciation of

> The blows that a life of self-control
> Spares to strike for the common good
> That day, giving a loose to my soul,
> I spent on the unimportant wood.

The poet even risks a little conceit in describing the season:

> Be glad of water, but don't forget
> The lurking frost in the earth beneath
> That will steal forth after the sun is set
> And show on the water its crystal teeth. [112]

These stanzas establish the character of the speaker so that the generalization which he utters in the end is dramatically justified —it is in character and in tone.

The generalization states a doctrine which I admire, and I have suggested the devices used by the poet to provide a dramatic frame for it. It may not be invidious therefore to point out that it is made finally in the mode of prose rather than in terms of symbol. The same censure applies to "Birches," and more severely still, to "Mending Wall." Frost prefers to dilute his poetry in contrast to the poets treated earlier in this study; and if dilution will account for his greater popularity, it will also indicate why he fails to realize full dramatic intensity. Compare with the conclusion to "Two Tramps in Mud Time" the "generalization" with which Yeats concludes "Among School Children":

> Labor is blossoming or dancing where
> The body is not bruised to pleasure soul,
> Nor beauty born out of its own despair,
> Nor blear-eyed wisdom out of midnight oil.
> O chestnut tree, great rooted blossomer,
> Are you the leaf, the blossom or the bole?
> O body swayed to music, O brightening glance,
> How can we know the dancer from the dance?

At his best, of course, Frost does not philosophize. The anecdote is absorbed into symbol. The method of indirection operates fully: the sense of realistic detail, the air of casual comment, are employed to build up and intensify a serious effect.

Consider "The Wood-Pile," for example. The poem is ostensibly the account of a winter walk, and, on the surface, the poem is as rambling and directionless as the walk. On the walk the poet scares up a bird, which is afraid of him and keeps flying on ahead:

> He thought that I was after him for a feather—
> The white one in his tail; like one who takes
> Everything said as personal to himself. [113]

(The bird becomes a New England character just as the colt in "The Runaway" becomes a New England urchin.) Finally, the walker comes upon the abandoned woodpile itself:

> Clematis
> Had wound strings round and round it like a bundle.
> What held it though on one side was a tree
> Still growing, and on one a stake and prop,
> These latter about to fall.

But the woodpile is burning and therefore warming the frozen swamp (rotting is oxidation, a kind of burning). Nature has picked up the abandoned task and is completing it. Nothing is lost. This is the point of the poem, but it is suggested merely. The poet does not even make it the central aspect of the thought with which he concludes the poem: What sort of person would go to the trouble of cutting and cording wood, only to leave it to warm the frozen swamp? [114]

☙ MALCOLM COWLEY[6]

1

Robert Frost has been heaped with more official and academic honors than any other American poet, living or dead. Although he was never graduated from college, having left Dartmouth after two months and Harvard after two years (and more credit to his dogged independence), he holds by the last count seventeen honorary degrees. He was twice made a Master of Arts (by Amherst and Michigan), three times a Doctor of the Humanities (by Vermont, Wesleyan and St. Lawrence) and twelve times a Doctor of Letters (by Yale, Middlebury, Bowdoin, New Hampshire, Columbia, Williams, Dartmouth, Bates, Pennsylvania, Harvard, Colorado and Princeton). He has been chosen as a Phi Beta Kappa poet by Tufts, William and Mary, Harvard (twice) and Columbia. He has been a professor at Amherst; a poet in residence and a fellow in letters at Michigan; a Charles Eliot Norton professor, a Ralph Waldo Emerson fellow and a fellow in American civilization at Harvard, all these being fairly lucrative appointments. He has been awarded four Pulitzer Prizes, one more than E. A. Robinson and two more than Stephen Vincent Benét, the only other poets to be named more than once. He has also received the Loines Prize for poetry, the Mark Twain medal, the gold medal of the National Institute of Arts and Letters and the silver medal of the Poetry Society of America. His work has been the subject of at least two full-length critical studies, many brochures, pamphlets, bibliographies and a memorial volume, "Recognition of Robert Frost," not to mention hundreds of essays which, with some discordant notes in the early years, have ended as a vast diapason of praise.

And Frost deserves all these honors, both for his poetry in itself and for a long career devoted to the art of verse. In a country where poets go to seed, he has kept his talent ready to produce perfect blossoms (together with some that are misshapen

---

[6] "Frost: A Dissenting Opinion," *New Republic*, CXI (September 11 and 18, 1944), 312-313, 345-347. The division of the article for periodical publication is here indicated by the numerals 1 and 2.

or overgrown). It is a pleasure to name over the poems of his youth and age that become more vivid in one's memory with each new reading: the dramatic dialogues like "The Death of the Hired Man" and "The Witch of Coös," besides half a dozen others almost equally good; the descriptions or narrations that turn imperceptibly into Aesop's fables, like "The Grindstone" and "Cow in Apple Time"; and, best of all, the short lyrics like "The Pasture," "Now Close the Windows," "The Sound of the Trees," "Fire and Ice," "Stopping by Woods on a Snowy Evening" (always a favorite with anthologists), "To Earthward," "Tree at My Window," "Acquainted with the Night," "Neither out Far Nor in Deep," "Beech," "Willful Homing," "Come In" . . . and I could easily add to the list. One of his best lyrics was written in 1892, when Frost was a freshman at Dartmouth; three or four others were included in his latest book, "A Witness Tree," published just fifty years later; and these recent poems show more skill and density of expression than almost anything he had written before. This same volume and the one that preceded it— "A Further Range," published in 1936—also contain bad poems that have been almost equally admired: long monologues in pedestrian blank verse, spoken as if from a cracker barrel among the clouds, and doggerel anecdotes directed (or rather, indirected) against the New Deal; but a poet has the right to be judged by his best work, and Frost at his best has added to our little store of authentic poetry.

If in spite of this I still say that there is a case against him and room for a dissenting opinion, perhaps I chiefly mean that there is a case against the zealous admirers who are not content to take the poet for what he is, but insist on using him as a sort of banner for their own moral or political crusades.

We have lately been watching the growth in this country of a narrow nationalism that has spread from politics into literature (although its literary adherents are usually not political isolationists). They demand, however, that American literature should be affirmative, optimistic, uncritical and "truly of this nation." They have been looking round for a poet to exalt; and Frost, through no fault of his own (but chiefly through the weaker qualities of his work), has been adopted as their symbol. Some of the honors heaped on him are less poetic than political. He is being praised too often and with too great vehemence by people who don't like poetry. And the result is that his honors shed very little of their luster on other poets, who in turn feel none of the pride in his achievements that a battalion feels, for example, when one of its officers is cited for outstanding services. Instead Frost is depicted by his admirers as a sort of Sunday-school paragon, a saint among miserable sinners. His common sense and strict Americanism are used as an excuse for berating and belittling other poets, who have supposedly fallen into the sins of pessimism, obscurity, obscenity and yielding to foreign influences; we even hear of their treachery to the American dream. Frost, on the other hand, is depicted as loyal, autochthonous and almost aboriginal. We are told not only that he is "the purest classical poet of America today"—and there is some truth in Gorham B. Munson's early judgment—but also that he is "the one great American poet of our time" and "the only living New Englander in the great tradition, fit to be placed beside Emerson, Hawthorne and Thoreau."

But when Frost is so placed and measured, his stature seems greatly diminished; it is almost as if a tough little Morgan horse, the best of its breed, had been judged by the standards that apply to Clydesdales and Percherons. Height, breadth and strength: he falls short in all these qualities of the great New Englanders. And the other quality for which he is often praised, his utter faithfulness to the New England spirit, is not one of the virtues they knowingly cultivated. They realized that the New England spirit, when it stands alone, is inclined to be narrow and arithmetical. It has reached its finest growth only when cross-fertilized with alien philosophies.

Hinduism, Sufism, Fourierism and German Romanticism: each of these doctrines contributed its own share to [312] the New England renaissance of the 1850's. Even Thoreau, who died almost in sight of his birthplace, said that he had traveled much in Concord; he spoke of bathing his intellect "in the stupendous and cosmogonal philosophy of the Bhagvat-Geeta. . . . The pure Walden water," he said, "is mingled with the sacred water of the Ganges." And Hawthorne, who told us that "New England is quite as large a lump of earth as my heart can really take in," was eager for any new ideas that might help to explain the nature of New Englanders as individuals or as members of society. The books he borrowed from the Salem Athenaeum during the ten lonely years he spent at home included the complete works, in French, of Rousseau, Voltaire (several times), Pascal, Racine (several times) and the "Essais" of Montaigne, as well as a great number of volumes on science, philosophy, general history and the past of New England. Some of his weaker contemporaries were quite unbalanced by the foreign learning with which they overloaded their minds; but the stronger ones assimilated everything and, in the end, reasserted their own New England natures, which had become immensely richer.

And even Frost, as purely Yankee as his character seems today, was partly formed by his three years abroad. The turning point in his life was when he sold his first New Hampshire farm (which his grandfather had bought for him on condition that he live there at least ten years) and when, in 1912, his wife said, "Let's go to England and live under thatch." In England he made the reputation that enabled him to continue his career as a poet (and also as a "poet in residence"). In England, too, he had the experience of meeting other poets who understood what he was trying to say: Lascelles Abercrombie, Rupert Brooke, Wilfred Wilson Gibson and Edward Thomas. They were willing to learn from him, and Frost, in a sense, learned even more from them: that is, he learned to abandon the conventional language of the Late Victorians and to use his own speech without embarrassment. It is interesting to compare "A Boy's Will," published in London but written in New Hampshire before his English journey, with "Mountain Interval," published after his return to this country in 1915 but written chiefly in England. The poems in "A Boy's Will" gave his own picture of the world, but in the language of the genteel poets; they were full of "maidens pale," "sweet pangs" and "airy dalliance." The poems written in the English countryside used the language that is spoken north of Boston. Once it had been regarded as a mere dialect only to be used in ballads like "Skipper Ireson's Ride" and in satirical comments like "The Bigelow Papers"; but Frost in England had done what Hemingway would later do in Paris: he had raised his own idiom to the dignity of a literary language.

It was after his return that he carried the process further. Having learned to write New Hampshire, he also began to think New Hampshire, in the sense of accepting its older customs as immutable laws. But this subject of Frost as a social philosopher and, at his worst, a Calvin Coolidge of poetry is one that I should like to discuss next week. [313]

2

In spite of his achievements as a narrative and lyric poet— some of which I mentioned last week—there is a case against Robert Frost as a social philosopher in verse and as a representative of the New England tradition. He is too much walled in by the past. Unlike the great Yankees of an earlier age, he is opposed to innovations in art, ethics, science, industry or politics. Thus, in one of his longer blank-verse monologues, he bridles when he hears a "New York alec" discussing Freudian psychology, which Frost dismisses as "the new school of the pseudo-phallic." Elsewhere he objects to researches in animal behavior (which he calls "instituting downward comparisons"), to new inventions (saying that ingenuity should be held in check) and even to the theory of evolution—or at least he ridicules one farmer who speaks of it admiringly, whereas he sympathizes with another who stops him on the road to say:

> The trouble with the Mid-Victorians
> Seems to have been a man named John L. Darwin.

New ideas seem worse to him if they come from abroad, and worst of all if they come from Russia. He is continually declaiming against the Russians of all categories: the pessimistic Russians, the revolutionary Russians, the collectivistic Russians, the five-year-planning Russians: he seems to embrace them all in a global and historical dislike that extends from Dostoevsky to Dnieperstroy. He is horrified by the thought that New England might be exposed to the possibility of adopting any good or bad feature of the Russian program. Thus, after reading about a project for rural rehabilitation, he hastened to write:

> It is in the news that all these pitiful kin
> Are to be bought out and mercifully gathered in
> To live in villages next to the theatre and store
> Where they won't have to think for themselves any more;
> While greedy good-doers, beneficent beasts of prey,
> Swarm over their lives enforcing benefits

That are calculated to soothe them out of their wits,
And by teaching them how to sleep the sleep all day,
Destroy their sleeping at night the ancient way.

Sometimes Frost decides that it would be a relief "To put these people at one stroke out of their pain"—these people being the marginal farmers; then next day he wonders how it would be if someone offered to put an end to his own troubles. The upshot is that he proposes to do nothing whatever, being satisfied with the New England countryside as it is—or rather, as it was in his early manhood—and outraged by anyone who tries to improve it.

Yet there are other poems in which he suggests that his faithfulness to "the ancient way" is more a matter of habit than conviction. In "The Black Cottage," he remembers an old woman who had lost her husband in the Civil War and who used to say (in her "quaint phrase," as Frost calls it) that all men were created free and equal. The old woman was also an orthodox Christian, and her presence in church kept the minister from changing any phrases in the Creed. The minister says, recalling "her old tremulous bonnet in the pew":

I'm just as glad she made me keep hands off,
For, dear me, why abandon a belief
Merely because it ceases to be true.
Cling to it long enough, and not a doubt
It will turn true again.

Although the minister is speaking, he seems to express Frost's attitude toward the old New England standards. The poet is more conventional than convinced, more concerned with prudence than with virtue, and very little concerned with sin or suffering; you might say that he is more Puritan, or even prudish, than he is Christian. All the figures in his poems are decently draped; all the love affairs (except in a very late narrative, "The Subverted Flower") are etherealized or intellectualized; and although he sometimes refers to very old adulteries, it is only after they have been wrapped in brown paper and locked away in cupboards. On the other hand, there is little in his work to suggest Christian charity or universal brotherhood under God. He wants us to understand once and for all that he is not his brother's keeper:

> I have none of the tenderer-than-thou
> Collectivistic regimenting love
> With which the modern world is being swept

—and the ancient world was also swept, in the first centuries after Christ. There is one of his narratives, "Two Tramps in Mud Time," that has often been praised for the admirable lesson with which it ends; and yet a professor told me not long ago that his classes always seemed vaguely uncomfortable when they heard it read aloud. It was first published in 1934, and it deals with what seems to have been an incident of the depression years. The poet tells us that he was working in his dooryard on an April day between winter and spring; he was splitting great blocks of straight-grained beech with a lively sense of satisfaction. Two tramps came walking down the muddy road. One of them said, "Hit them hard," and then lingered by the roadside, suggesting wordlessly that he might take the poet's job for pay. The poet assumed that they had spent the winter in a lumber camp, that they were now unemployed and that they had slept "God knows where last night." In life the meeting may have had a different sequel. Perhaps the poet explained to the homeless men that he liked to split his own wood, but that he had other work for them to do; or perhaps he invited them into the kitchen for a slab of home-baked bread spread thick with apple butter. In the poem, however, he lets them walk away without a promise or a penny; and perhaps that explains why a college class—west of the Alleghanies, at least—cannot hear it read without feeling uneasy. Instead of helping these men who wanted to work, Frost turns to the reader with a sound but rather sententious sermon on the ethical value of the chopping block: [345]

> But yield who will to their separation,
> My object in living is to unite
> My avocation and my vocation
> As my two eyes make one in sight.
> Only where love and need are one,
> And the work is play for mortal stakes,
> Is the deed ever really done
> For Heaven and the future's sakes.

The meter and tone of the passage remind us of another narrative poem written in New England almost a hundred years before; but "The Vision of Sir Launfal" had a different moral to point:

> Not what we give but what we share,
> For the gift without the giver is bare;
> Who gives himself with his alms feeds three,
> Himself, his hungering neighbor and me.

What Frost sets before us is an ideal, not of charity or brotherhood, but of separateness. "Keep off each other and keep each other off," he tells us in "Build Soil." "We're too unseparate out among each other. . . . Steal away and stay away." In some of his poems he faintly suggests Emerson, and yet he is preaching only half the doctrine of self-reliance, which embraced the community as well as the individual. Emerson said, for example, "He only who is able to stand alone is qualified for society," thus implying that the self-reliant individual was to use his energies for social ends. Frost, on the other hand, makes no distinction between separateness and self-centeredness. In his poems, fine as the best of them are, the social passions of the great New Englanders are diverted into narrower channels. One cannot imagine him thundering against the Fugitive Slave Law, like Emerson; or rising like Thoreau to defend John Brown after the Harper's Ferry raid; or even conducting a quietly persistent campaign against brutality on American ships, as Hawthorne did when he was consul at Liverpool. He is concerned chiefly with himself and his near neighbors, or rather with the Yankees among his neighbors (for although his section of New England is largely inhabited by Poles and French Canadians, there are only two poems in which these foreigners are mentioned). He says when splitting his straight-grained beech blocks:

> The blows that a life of self-control
> Spares to strike for the common good
> That day, giving a loose to my soul,
> I spent on the unimportant wood;

—and one feels that these blows might symbolize the inward or backward turning of energies in a region that once had wider horizons.

And Frost does not strive toward greater depth to compensate for what he lacks in breadth; he does not strike far inward into the wilderness of human nature. It is true that he often talks about the need for inwardness. He says, for example, in "Build Soil," which for all its limitations of doctrine is the best of his long philosophical poems and perhaps the only one worth preserving:

> We're always too much out or too much in.
> At present from a cosmical dilation
> We're so much out that the odds are against
> Our ever getting inside in again;

—yet still he sets limits on the exploration of himself, as he sets them on almost every other human activity; here again he displays the sense of measure and decorum that puts him in the classical, or rather the neo-classical, tradition. He is always building defenses against the infinite, walls that stand "Between too much and me." In the woods, there is a pile of rocks and an iron stake to mark the limit of his land; and here too:

> One tree, by being deeply wounded,
> Has been impressed as Witness Tree
> And made commit to memory
> My proof of being not unbounded.

The woods play a curious part in Frost's poems; they seem to be his symbol for the uncharted country within ourselves, full of possible beauty, but also full of horror. From the woods at dusk, you might hear the hidden music of the brook, "a slender, tinkling fall"; or you might see wood creatures, a buck and a doe, looking at you over the stone fence that marks the limit of the pasture lot. But you don't cross the fence, except in dreams; and then, instead of brook or deer, you are likely to meet a strange Demon rising "from his wallow to laugh." And so, for fear of the Demon, and also because of your moral obligations, you merely stand at the edge of the woods to listen:

> Far in the pillared dark
> Thrush music went—
> Almost like a call to come in
> To the dark and lament.
>
> But no, I was out for stars:
> I would not come in.
> I meant not even if asked,
> And I hadn't been.

But Hawthorne before him, timid and thin and conventional as he was in many of his tales, still plucked up his courage and ventured into the inner wilderness; and Conrad Aiken's poems (to mention one example of New England work today) are written almost wholly from within that haunted mid-region. To explore the real horrors of the mind is a long tradition in American letters, one that goes back to our first professional novelist, Charles Brockden Brown. He said in one of his letters, quoted in a footnote by Van Wyck Brooks, "You, you tell me, are one of those who would rather travel into the mind of a plowman than into the interior of Africa. I confess myself of your way of thinking." The same tendency was continued by Poe and Melville and Henry James, and it extends in an almost unbroken line into the late work of Hemingway and Faulkner. But Frost, even in his finest lyrics, is content to stop outside the woods, either in the thrush-haunted dusk or on a snowy evening:

> The woods are lovely, dark and deep,
> But I have promises to keep,
> And miles to go before I sleep,
> And miles to go before I sleep.

If he does not strike far inward, neither does he follow the other great American tradition (extending from Whitman through Dos Passos) of standing on a height to observe the panorama of nature and society. Let us say that he is a poet neither of the mountains nor of the woods, although he lives among both, but rather of the hill pastures, [346] the intervales, the dooryard in autumn with the leaves swirling, the closed house shaking in the winter storms (and who else has described these scenes more accurately, in more lasting colors?). In the same way, he is not the poet of New England in its great days, or in its late-nineteenth-century decline (except in some of his earlier poems); he is rather a poet who celebrates the diminished but prosperous and self-respecting New England of the tourist home and the antique shop in the abandoned gristmill. And the praise heaped on Frost in recent years is somehow connected in one's mind with the search for ancestors and authentic old furniture. You imagine a saltbox cottage restored to its original lines; outside it a wellsweep preserved for its picturesque quality, even though there is also an electric pump; at the doorway a coach lamp wired and polished; inside the house a set of Hitchcock chairs, a Salem rocker, willowware plates and Sandwich glass; and, on the tip-top table, carefully dusted, a first edition of Robert Frost. [347]

❧ GEORGE F. WHICHER[7]

In his unexpected and delightful poetic playlet, *A Masque of Reason*, Robert Frost represents the Old Testament figure of Job as welcoming the approach of what he thinks may well be the Day of Judgment with the words:

> Here's where I lay aside
> My varying opinion of myself
> And come to rest in an official verdict.

It is now something over fifty years since the earliest known of Frost's poems was written. For approximately two decades of that time he served an apprenticeship to his art not less exacting because self-administered, publishing little, but testing himself to make sure that he had something to say and a voice of his own with which to say it. Since 1913, when *A Boy's Will* was issued in London, he has come forward at deliberate intervals with gatherings of well-seasoned poems, seven books in all, not counting volumes of selected or collected poems. From almost the first he has been recognized as one of the master-singers of our age. He has received almost every form of public recognition that could be given to a man of letters, except the Nobel Prize for literature. Now that he has completed his seventieth year, rich in honors and the regard of friends, it would seem possible to anticipate the tenor of the official verdict that posterity will declare upon his work as a whole.

Why has Frost survived so well? The sources of his power do [405] not lie in his being the spokesman of any tendency or movement. He has never been committed to any program. He has faced contemporary currents of thought with a tough-minded skepticism. He has resisted classification. At one time or another he has been factory-hand, farmer, journalist, and teacher,

[7] From "Frost at Seventy." Reprinted from *American Scholar*, XIV (Autumn 1945), 405-414. Copyright 1945 by the United Chapters of Phi Beta Kappa. By permission of the publishers.

but the one activity to which he has wholeheartedly devoted his energies is the writing of poetry. He has made common cause with no group or class except poets. Though deeply attached to neighborhood and nation, he has never been willing to acknowledge any allegiance to the particular age in which he lives. In that respect he is different from the literary set whom it is proper to label modernists.

There may have been moments when poets did not have to choose between being humanly complete and being contemporary, but our distracted time is not one of them. The period of Frost's poetic activity has coincided almost exactly with the inter-Armageddon era between the inconclusive World War of 1914-18 and its global aftermath. During these years, while the United States was all unconsciously becoming one of the most powerful nations in existence, many voices were busily proclaiming that the civilization of the West was verging to a decline. Or if not declining, it was about to undergo a cataclysmic change of direction. A phase of culture originating in the sixteenth century and culminant in the nineteenth had, we were informed, run its course, and its outworn institutions—protestantism, democracy, capitalism, and science—were doomed to swift decay. A widespread conviction of defeat and hopelessness set the stage for a period of decadent art. . . . [406]

Frost's distinction is precisely that he has maintained during a time of general disillusionment his instinctive belief in the tradition that lies at the core of our national being, the tradition of liberal democracy.

> As long as the Declaration guards
> My right to be equal in number of cards,
> It is nothing to me who runs the Dive.

No reader of his poems can suppose that Frost's serenity is the product of an easy optimism. He has known what it is to feel himself swept and shaken, he has been acquainted with dark hours, he has experienced poverty and injustice. His power of neighborly sympathy with others is attested beyond the possibility of contravention in "The Death of the Hired Man," "A Servant to Servants," "The Self-Seeker," "The Hill Wife," and " 'Out, Out'—" among many other poems. But Frost is more than a mass of sensibilities.

> I have a mind myself and recognize
> Mind where I meet with it in any guise.

He has firmness of judgment and a sense of history. He has never expected to find this world an easy place for man to save his soul in. Programs for the promulgation of social justice from [408] Geneva, Moscow, or Washington have not roused his enthusiasm. His social philosophy is expressed in an epigram that will bear long pondering: "The opposite of Utopia is civilization." Edmund Burke would have understood this, even if the editors of the *New Republic* do not.

It is a trifle on the ironic side that the same magazine which was the first to recognize Frost when he returned to this country, a little-known American poet who had just had two books somewhat obscurely published in London, should be the first publication to sound a note of disparagement in the fullness of his powers. Yet it has so happened. In two issues of the *New Republic* a year ago, one of the contributing editors, Malcolm Cowley, compiled what he considered the case against Frost as a social philosopher and, at his worst, "a Calvin Coolidge of poetry."

The first count in the indictment is that Frost has become, or has been taken by some of his admirers to be, the symbol of a narrow nationalism. The color given to this charge exists largely in the eye of the critic. Frost is a deeply patriotic American, and is genuinely concerned to promote what may be called the cultural integrity of the United States. His point of view is developed at some length in the poem called "Build Soil," which Mr. Cowley professes to admire in itself, though he does not seem to be able to stomach some of its applications. Frost's attitude is not essentially different from that of William Ellery Channing a century ago, when he wrote in his "Remarks on National Literature":

> We cannot admit the thought, that this country is to be only a repetition of the old world. . . . We are accustomed to estimate nations by their creative energies, and we shall blush for our country, if, in circumstances so peculiar, original, and creative, it shall satisfy itself with a passive reception and mechanical reiteration of the thoughts of strangers.

It is not essentially different from the attitude of Emerson when he asked at the beginning of "Nature" the key question of his philosophy: "Why should not we also enjoy an original relation to the universe?"

If to hope and desire that the United States should display a positive energy of mind and spirit equivalent to its physical [409] energy is narrowly nationalistic, then Frost is guilty of a narrow nationalism along with every other well-wisher of this country from the time when Michael Drayton sent off the first Virginian colonists with the prayer, not that they might carry Shakespeare, Sidney, and Spenser to the wilderness, but that they might in time crown with laurel of the New World a poet "that may sing there."

But, objects Mr. Cowley, Frost cannot be considered to belong to the great New England tradition, for Emerson, Thoreau, and the rest were receptive in their time of alien philosophies. They read the scriptures of the East, and their minds were fertilized by contact with oriental influences. Frost, on the contrary, has not welcomed Freudianism with appropriate solemnity, he has recorded the remark of a New Hampshire farmer that many of the world's difficulties seem to be due to a man named "John L. Darwin," and he has even poked fun at the earnest efforts of those who seek to write the Russian novel in America.

We have here a striking example of how a little knowledge can be made to pay large dividends in talking points. It is a matter of textbook information that Emerson, Thoreau, and Alcott read everything they could lay their hands on from the literatures of India, China, and Persia, but it is yet to be shown that their opinions were changed one iota by what they read. They responded to the wisdom of the East as the Concord farmer responded to Plato when he remarked that the book seemed to contain "a good many of my own idees." From their oriental excursions the Transcendentalists returned with notebooks filled with sentences that could be used to support and illustrate their previously formed convictions. Of the deeper essence of Eastern mysticism they learned practically nothing.

No, Emerson who advised the American scholar to keep away from libraries except in moments of failing inspiration is not a happy choice in this connection. No doubt books from abroad were much rarer in New England a century ago than they are today and so were more eagerly sought. Our grandfathers did not have to choose, like the young couple pictured in the *New Yorker* some years back, between having a baby or reading [410] Pareto. But from what Frost's poems manifest of his awareness of philosophy, literature, travel, history, and science, I should say that his only superior among the Transcendentalists was the omnivorous Theodore Parker, who seemed to his contemporaries to have read everything. What Mr. Cowley regards as Frost's hostility to novel ideas might otherwise be described as intellectual toughness of fiber, a willingness to test out ideas by playful indirection rather than to swallow them whole.

So far we have encountered what perhaps is no more than the normal divergence of view between a poet interested in immediate human values and a social scientist trained to appraise human data from an impersonal and generalized standpoint. But when Mr. Cowley goes on to claim that Frost is not interested in universal brotherhood under God and is therefore deficient in human charity, he makes a charge which if true would be serious. In one sense it is conspicuously not true. The neighborliness of Frost has been from the first a keynote of his poetry too obvious to be missed. When Mr. Cowley accuses him of small enthusiasm for human brotherhood, therefore, he must have reference to mass programs of brotherhood by fiat and ballyhoo. But let us look at the evidence.

The case seems to rest on passages selected here and there from Frost's poems and considered without reference to their tone and context. A habit of hunting through books in this fashion to pounce on illustrations of a preconceived idea is almost certain to lead to serious misinterpretation. Mr. Cowley, for instance, detaches from their setting the lines:

> I have none of the tenderer-than-thou
> Collectivistic regimenting love
> With which the modern world is being swept—

and remarks that the ancient world was also swept by the same "regimenting" love in the first centuries after Christ, thus by one of the longest intellectual leaps on record identifying Communism with Christianity and so arriving at the conclusion that Frost lacks Christian charity. But in what connection do the lines occur? They belong in a playful poem called "A Considerable Speck" dealing with an almost microscopic insect on the [411] poet's writing paper. To take them out of that connection is to ignore what is the most important thing about them—the tone in which they are spoken, the twinkle in the eye at the conjunction of a momentous declaration and a trivial occasion. To take the lines in an absolute sense is poppycock. One might as well argue that when Burns wrote:

> The best-laid schemes o'mice an' men
> Gang aft agley,

he was warning us against a planned economy and should be discredited as an "economic royalist."

But a far worse example of missing the poet's whole intention occurs when Mr. Cowley analyzes for his purposes the fine narrative piece called "Two Tramps in Mud Time." His summary of the action will recall the poem:

The poet tells us that he was working in the dooryard on an April day between winter and spring; he was splitting great blocks of straight-grained beech with a lively sense of satisfaction. Two tramps came walking down the muddy road. One of them said, "Hit them hard," and then lingered by the roadside, suggesting wordlessly that he might take the poet's job for pay. The poet assumed that they had spent the winter in a lumber camp, that they were now unemployed and that they had slept "God knows where last night."

So far the skeleton of the poem at least is fairly represented. But at this point Mr. Cowley diverges from the poem to explain what the proper response to the experience of meeting two unemployed men should be, and to blame the poet for not giving it, but instead ending the poem with what the critic chooses to call a "rather sententious sermon on the ethical value of the chopping block." Let us recall the lines:

> But yield who will to their separation,
> My object in living is to unite
> My avocation and my vocation
> As my two eyes make one in sight.
> Only where love and need are one,
> And the work is play for mortal stakes,
> Is the deed ever really done
> For Heaven and the future's sakes.

124

It will be just as well to take our bearings. When Wordsworth in "Resolution and Independence" described his meeting with [412] a feeble and aged leech-gatherer on a lonely moor, he chose to make of the incident a tribute to man's indomitable endurance. The poet, gloomy over his personal prospects and in a dither of despair at the way things were going in France, found consolation in the discovery that one so much worse off than he could take a hopeless situation in his stride and go uncomplainingly about his affairs. Are we to say that Wordsworth blundered by not rushing home to write a plea for old-age pensions? No, the stock response of the social worker has its value in the scheme of things, but it has small value in poetry. The poet as poet is concerned with the meaning of an experience to an individual at a particular time and place, not with its bearing on problems of society at large.

And now to return to Frost's poem. Notice what is not brought out in Mr. Cowley's summary, that after the scene is set in the first two stanzas, three more stanzas are devoted to a leisurely and lovely description of the April weather and the poet's surroundings. These things conspire to make the moment

The time when most I loved my task.

And the threat that the occupation he so deeply enjoys may be taken from him by the necessities of the casual passers-by only makes him cherish it the more. For Mr. Cowley's peace of mind, remember that the person speaking is not a Long Island millionaire taking week-end exercise, but a poet engaged in failing at farming, a poet who was never very far above the bare subsistence level himself. There is too a certain pride of craftsmanship suggested when the poet remarks of the two tramps,

Except as a fellow handled an ax,
They had no way of knowing a fool.

The poem thus becomes a discussion of the philosophy of employment, not prejudged but freshly examined in relation to a personal experience. Are we to say that need is the only justification for labor, and think of jobs, in the modern fashion, merely as excuses for handing out so many livelihoods? To do so is to rob man of two precious illusions—first, the idea that his job is worth doing for its own sake, and second, that it is worth doing [413] as a challenge to the doer's skill and stamina. When Mr. Cowley has understood the double paradox in the line:

And the work is play for mortal stakes,

he will have a key to a poem which he is a long way from comprehending at present.

When Mr. Cowley goes on to say that Robert Frost has never been willing to venture into the inner wilderness or to explore the real horrors of the mind in the wake of Charles Brockden Brown, Poe, Hawthorne, Melville, Henry James, Conrad Aiken, and the later Hemingway and Faulkner, I readily agree that the poet does not belong in that gallery. But I marvel at the critic who can recognize only one portal to the inner life, and that a narrow Gothic one. Such poems of Frost's as "Home Burial," "The Fear," "An Old Man's Winter Night," "Paul's Wife," "Maple," "Tree at My Window," "Acquainted with the Night," and "Desert Places," to name only those that first come to mind, have enough to say of human inwardness to prevent Frost from being regarded as merely a phenomenon of hillside pastures.

Near the beginning of his career Frost was taken to task by Amy Lowell for writing in *North of Boston* what she persisted in regarding as "a very sad book." With her genius for missing all but the obvious she overlooked the implicit humor that is rarely lacking in his poems. Reviewers of his latest book, on the other hand, seem often aware of nothing but the humor, ignoring the range of reflectiveness beneath the surface. But regardless of passing fashions in criticism, the reading public has accepted Frost as the poet of our time and country; and the ultimate test of a poet is not, as Job whimsically remarks, how he treats the poor, but what kind of artistic performance he is capable of giving. By that pragmatic test over a span of more than thirty years Frost has demonstrated a capacity to wear well. It seems likely that the leading position he now holds among contemporary poets will become still more marked in coming years. [414]

Besides the Frost that everybody knows there is one whom no one even talks about. Everybody knows what the regular Frost is: the one living poet who has written *good* poems that ordinary readers like without any trouble and understand without any trouble; the conservative editorialist and self-made apothegm-joiner, full of dry wisdom and free, complacent, Yankee enterprise; the Farmer-Poet—this is an imposing private role perfected for public use, a sort of Olympian Will Rogers out of *Tangle-wood Tales;* and, last or first of all, Frost is the standing, speaking reproach to any other good modern poet: "If Frost can write poetry that's just as easy as Longfellow you can too—you do too." It is this "easy" side of Frost that is most attractive to academic readers, who are eager to canonize any modern poet who condemns in example the modern poetry which they condemn in precept; and it is this side that has helped to get him neglected or depreciated by intellectuals—the reader of Eliot or Auden usually dismisses Frost as something inconsequentially good that *he* knew all about long ago. Ordinary readers think Frost the greatest poet alive, and love some of his best poems almost as much as they love some of his worst ones. He seems to them a sensible, tender, humorous poet who knows all about trees and farms and folks in New England, and still has managed to get an individualistic, fairly optimistic, thoroughly American philosophy out of what he knows; there's something reassuring about his poetry, [26] they feel—almost like prose. Certainly there's nothing hard or odd or gloomy about it.

These views of Frost, it seems to me, come either from not knowing his poems well enough or from knowing the wrong poems too well. Frost's best-known poems, with a few exceptions, are not his best poems at all; when you read (say) the selections in Untermeyer, you are getting a good synopsis of the ordinary idea of Frost and a bad misrepresentation of the real Frost. It would be hard to make a novel list of Eliot's best poems,

---

[8] "The Other Frost," *Poetry and the Age*, New York: Vintage, 1955, pp. 26-33. Reprinted by permission of Alfred A. Knopf, Inc. Copyright 1947, 1953 by Randall Jarrell.

but one can make a list of ten or twelve of Frost's best poems that is likely to seem to anybody too new to be true. Here it is: "The Witch of Coös," "Neither Out Far Nor In Deep," "Directive," "Design," "A Servant to Servants," "Provide, Provide," "Home Burial," "Acquainted with the Night," "The Pauper Witch of Grafton" (mainly for its ending), "An Old Man's Winter Night," "The Gift Outright," "After Apple-Picking," "Desert Places," and "The Fear."

Nothing I say about these poems can make you see what they are like, or what the Frost that matters most is like; if you read them you will see. "The Witch of Coös" is the best thing of its kind since Chaucer. "Home Burial" and "A Servant to Servants" are two of the most moving and appalling dramatic poems ever written; and how could lyrics be more ingeniously and conclusively merciless than "Neither Out Far Nor In Deep" or "Design"? or more grotesquely and subtly and mercilessly disenchantting than the tender "An Old Man's Winter Night"? or more unsparingly truthful than "Provide, Provide"? And so far from being obvious, optimistic, orthodox, many of these poems are extraordinarily subtle and strange, poems which express an attitude that, at its most extreme, makes pessimism seem a hopeful evasion; they begin with a flat [27] and terrible reproduction of the evil in the world and end by saying: It's so; and there's nothing you can do about it; and if there were, would *you* ever do it? The limits which existence approaches and falls back from have seldom been stated with such bare composure.

Frost's virtues are extraordinary. No other living poet has written so well about the actions of ordinary men: his wonderful dramatic monologues or dramatic scenes come out of a knowledge of people that few poets have had, and they are written in a verse that uses, sometimes with absolute mastery, the rhythms of actual speech. Particularly in his blank verse there is a movement so characteristic, so unmistakably and overwhelmingly Frost's, that one feels about it almost as Madame de Guermantes felt about those Frans Halses at Haarlem: that if you caught just a glimpse of them, going by in the street-car, you would be able to tell they were something pretty unusual. It is easy to underestimate the effect of this exact, spaced-out, prosaic rhythm, whose objects have the tremendous strength—you find it in Hardy's best poems —of things merely put down and left to speak for themselves.

(Though Frost has little of Hardy's self-effacement, his matter-of-fact humility; Frost's tenderness, sadness, and humor are adulterated with vanity and a hard complacency.) Frost's seriousness and honesty; the bare sorrow with which, sometimes, things are accepted as they are, neither exaggerated nor explained away; the many, many poems in which there are real people with their real speech and real thoughts and real emotions—all this, in conjunction with so much subtlety and exactness, such classical understatement and restraint, makes the reader feel that he is not in a book but in a world, and a world that has in common with his own some of the things that are most [28] important in both. I don't need to praise anything so justly famous as Frost's observation of and empathy with everything in Nature from a hornet to a hillside; and he has observed his own nature, one person's random or consequential chains of thoughts and feelings and perceptions, quite as well. (And this person, in the poems, is not the "alienated artist" cut off from everybody who isn't, yum-yum, another alienated artist; he is someone like normal people only more so—a normal person in the less common and more important sense of *normal*.) The least crevice of the good poems is saturated with imagination, an imagination that expresses itself in the continual wit and humor and particularly of what is said, in the hand-hewn or hand-polished texture of its saying. The responsibility and seriousness of Frost's best work—his worst work has an irresponsible conceit, and indifference to everything but himself, that appalls one—are nowhere better manifested than in the organization of these poems: an organization that, in its concern for any involution or ramification that really belongs to its subject, and in its severity toward anything else, expresses that absorption into a subject that is prior even to affection. The organization of Frost's poems is often rather simple or—as people say—"old-fashioned." But, as people ought to know, very complicated organizations are excessively rare in poetry, although in our time a very complicated disorganization has been excessively common; there is more successful organization in "Home Burial" or "The Witch of Coös"—one feels like saying, in indignant exaggeration—than in the *Cantos* and *The Bridge* put together. These titles will remind anyone of what is scarcest in Frost: rhetoric and romance, hypnotic verbal excitement, Original Hart Crane. Frost's word-magic is generally of a quiet, sober, bewitching sort, though the contrasts he gets [29] from his greyed or unsaturated shades are often more satisfying to a thoughtful rhetorician than some dazzling arrangements of prismatic colors. Yet there are dazzling passages in Frost.

Frost has written, as everybody knows: "I never dared be radical when young/For fear it would make me conservative when old." This is about as truthful as it is metrical: Frost *was* radical when young—he was a very odd and very radical radical, a much more interesting sort than the standard *New Republic* brand—and now that he's old he's sometimes callously and unimaginatively conservative. Take his poems about the atomic bomb in *Steeple Bush;* these amount, almost, to a very old and a very successful man saying: "I've had my life—why should you worry about yours?" The man who called himself "the author/ Of several books against the world in general"; who said that he had learned from Marlowe's Mephistopheles to say his prayers, "Why this is Hell, nor am I out of it"; who said to Henry Hudson, drowned or frozen somewhere in Hudson's Bay: "You and I and the Great Auk"; who could be annoyed at a hornet for not recognizing him as "the exception I like to think I am in everything"; who in poems like "A Servant to Servants," "Home Burial," and "The Witch of Coös" had a final identifying knowledge of the deprived and dispossessed, the insulted and injured, that one matches in modern poetry only in Hardy—this poet is now, most of the time, an elder statesman like Baruch or Smuts, full of complacent wisdom and cast-iron whimsy. But of course there was always a good deal of this in the official role that Frost created for himself; one imagines Yeats saying about Frost, as Sarah Bernhardt said about Nijinsky: "I fear, I greatly fear, that I have just seen the greatest actor in the world."

Sometimes it is this public figure, this official role—[30] the Only Genuine Robert Frost in Captivity—that writes the poems, and not the poet himself; and then one gets a self-made man's political editorials, full of cracker-box philosophizing, almanac joke-cracking—of a snake-oil salesman's mysticism; one gets the public figure's relishing consciousness of himself, an astonishing constriction of imagination and sympathy; one gets sentimentality and whimsicality, an arch complacency, a complacent archness; and one gets Homely Wisdom till the cows come home. Often the later Frost makes demands on himself that are minimal: he uses a little wit and a little observation and a little sentiment to stuff —not very tight—a little sonnet; and it's not bad, but not good enough to matter, either. The extremely rare, extremely wonderful dramatic and narrative element that is more important than anything else in his early poetry almost disappears from his later poetry; in his later work the best poems are usually special-case, rather than all-out, full-scale affairs. The younger Frost is surrounded by his characters, living beings he has known or created; the older Frost is alone. But it is this loneliness that is responsible for the cold finality of poems like "Neither Out Far Nor In Deep" or "Design."

Frost's latest books deserve little more than a footnote, since they have had few of his virtues, most of his vices, and all of his tricks; the heathen who would be converted to Frost by them is hard to construct. *Steeple Bush* has one wonderful poem, "Directive"; a fairly good, dazzlingly heartless one, "The Ingenuities of Debt"; and nothing else that is not done better somewhere else in Frost. Most of the poems merely remind you, by their persistence in the mannerisms of what was genius, that they are the productions of someone who once, and somewhere else, was a great poet. But one stops for a long time at "Directive." [31]

A Masque of Mercy, though no great shakes—as you see, its style is catching—is a great improvement on the earlier *A Masque of Reason*, which is a frivolous, trivial, and bewilderingly corny affair, full of jokes inexplicable except as the contemptuous patter of an old magician certain that *he* can get away with anything in the world: *What fools these readers be!* Besides, Frost has long ago divorced reason for common sense, and is basking complacently in his bargain; consequently, when common sense has God justify His ways to Job by saying, "I was just showing off to Satan," the performance has the bleak wisdom of Calvin Coolidge telling you what life comes to at 2½%.

The plot of *A Masque of Mercy* is as simple as that of *Merope*, but it is a plot that is more likely to get Frost recognized as one more precursor of surrealism than it is to get him looked askance at as one of Arnold's Greeks. A bookstore-keeper named My Brother's Keeper has a wife named Jesse Bel; one night Jonah—who, having forgotten both his gourd and what God taught him by it, is feeling for New York City all the hatred that he used to feel for Nineveh—seeks refuge in the bookstore; after a little talk from Saint Paul (Jesse Bel's psychiatrist) and a lot of talk from Keeper (a character who develops so much that he finally develops into Robert Frost), Jonah comes to realize that "justice doesn't really matter."

Frost lavishes some care and a good deal more self-indulgence on this congenial subject. He has a thorough skepticism about that tame revenge, justice, and a cold certainty that nothing but mercy will do for *us*. What he really warms to is a rejection beyond either justice or mercy, and the most felt and moving part of his poem is the "unshaken recognition"—that is to say, the willing assertion—that [32]

> Our sacrifice, the best we have to offer,
> And not our worst nor second best, our best,
> Our very best, our lives laid down like Jonah's,
> Our lives laid down in war and peace, may not
> Be found acceptable in Heaven's sight.

To feel this Fear of God and to go ahead in spite of it, Frost says, is man's principal virtue, courage. He treats Paul very sympathetically, but gives him speeches that are ineffectual echoes of what he really said; and Frost makes about him that sorry old joke which finds that he "theologized Christ out of Christianity." Paul ends in jokes like this, Columbus in chains; these are the rewards of discovery. [33]

❦ LEONARD UNGER AND WILLIAM VAN O'CONNOR[9]

It is customary, and also accurate, to describe the poetry of Robert Frost as traditional and popular. As used here, these descriptive terms are close to each other in meaning. Frost's poetry, unlike that of such contemporaries as Eliot, Stevens, and the later Yeats, shows no marked departure from the poetic practices of the nineteenth century. Those influences which have shaped modernism—such as the free verse movement, the French symbolists, the seventeenth-century metaphysicals—have left no

[9] From *Poems for Study*, New York: Rinehart, 1953, pp. 593-594.

trace on the work of Frost. The average reader of poetry in the early decades of the twentieth century, with tastes and preconceptions determined by nineteenth-century poetry, found Frost not only intelligible and familiar but frequently simple and homely. These qualities have, no doubt, contributed to Frost's popularity.

But Frost has been no mere continuator of the nineteenth-century traditions. While preserving certain basic features, he has brought them up to date with the prevailing principles of his own time. It is interesting to note that many of the modern characteristics of Frost's poetry are also appropriate to the literary personality and poetic role which Frost has chosen and within which he has worked, that of the New England rural character. This role has made it possible for him to blend successfully the traditional and the contemporary. Frost has put into blank verse, couplets, and a variety of stanzas the dry and pithy quality of Yankee speech. Except for a few instances of poetic license and echoes of nineteenth-century tone in his earliest volume, *A Boy's Will*, he remains faithful to the spoken language of his own time. Frost's Yankee manner, with its mixture of playfulness and seriousness, its skepticism and habit of understatement, has paralleled the contemporary tendency toward indirection and irony. And his regionalism, with its rich stock of images, situations, and anecdotes, has provided him with an abundant source of metaphor and symbol.

If Frost's poetry has the qualities of homeliness and simplicity, it has these, not because they are inevitable, but because Frost has achieved them. It is possible to be misled by these qualities into the notion that his poems are simple in all respects. Actually the simplicity is an effect achieved by a skillful and controlled craftsmanship, and it is related to the technique of understatement (a device for concentration and subtle shading of meaning). Beneath the simplicity can be found an intellectuality of attitude, a discernible structure, and a highly developed figurative technique.

A recurring pattern of development is to be found in many of the poems. Frost often begins a poem by presenting some actual detail or circumstance and exploring the features of this material. Then, with a sustained playfulness of tone, an imaginative whimsicality is mixed with or succeeds the realistic comment until the actual material with which the poem began, whether pattern Frost handles the central metaphors of his [593] poems in image or situation, yields a meaningful metaphor. Within this a number of ways. At times he uses the metaphor as a transition to and in illustration of a general statement of idea, belief, or attitude. Examples of this procedure are "Birches" and "Two Tramps in Mud Time." At other times, usually in shorter lyrical poems, the shift into metaphor and then into statement is not obvious but rather a steady and uninterrupted development of the circumstantial materials until they take on a metaphorical or symbolical value. "Stopping by Woods on a Snowy Evening" and "For Once, Then, Something" are examples of such development. It is in these shorter poems that Frost's use of realistic materials and metaphorical technique is most successful. In these poems the developed meanings seem to inhere inevitably in the realistic images and situations, in the actual thing. In poems like "Birches," however, the relationship between thing and meaning seems mechanically contrived for the sake of the meaning. Instead of becoming meaningful while it remains vivid in the fullness of its own individuality, the thing becomes covered over with abstract meaning and loses its vividness. In such poems an element of didacticism is not wholly avoided, despite Frost's carefully sustained qualities of casualness and humor. Significantly, in these poems the metaphorical relationship is often weak. Frost himself has said that every metaphor breaks down somewhere, and that with metaphor it is "touch and go." That breaking point, that point of departure, is too conspicuous in poems like "Birches."

Perhaps that is why Frost handles these metaphors in so playful a tone and so tentative a manner. If we grant the weakness of the metaphor, we must at least admire the skillfulness with which Frost avoids the worst consequences. And whether or not they succeed by one standard, Frost's metaphors usually have freshness and charm. Even in those poems which are diffuse and discursive, there is a positive stylistic achievement, an unwavering appropriateness of tone. Where there is looseness of structure, that looseness is often a device contributing to the achieved tone. However, there are marked limitations to the tonal range within which Frost works and has his successes. One does not find intensity of language in Frost's poetry. Intensity is not characteristic of the Yankee manner. It is not produced by understatement, whimsy, and casualness. But while Frost does not commit himself to intensity, he can achieve concentration of meaning. [594]

✻ YVOR WINTERS[10]

Robert Frost is one of the most talented poets of our time, but I believe that his work is both overestimated and misunderstood; and it seems to me of the utmost importance that we should understand him with some accuracy. If we can arrive at a reasonably sound understanding of him, we can profit by his virtues without risk of acquiring his defects; and we may incidentally arrive at a better understanding of our present culture.

A popular poet is always a spectacle of some interest, for poetry in general is not popular; and when the popular poet is also within limits a distinguished poet, the spectacle is even more curious, for commonly it is bad poetry which is popular. When we encounter such a spectacle, we may be reasonably sure of finding certain social and historical reasons for the popularity. Frost is similar in his ways and attitudes and perceptions to a very large number of the more intelligent, if not the most intelligent, of his contemporaries: to the school teachers, the English professors, the more or less literate undergraduates, the journalists, and the casual readers of every class. These people are numerous and are in a position to perpetuate their ways and attitudes; this similarity therefore is worth examining.

Frost has been praised as a classical poet, but he is not classical in any sense which I can understand. Like many of his contemporaries, he is an Emersonian Romantic, although with certain mutings and modifications which I shall mention presently, and he has labeled himself as such with a good deal of care. He is a poet of the minor theme, the casual approach, and the discreetly eccentric attitude. When a reader calls Frost a classical poet, he probably means that Frost strikes him as a "natural" poet, a poet who somehow resembles himself and his neighbors;

---

[10] From "Robert Frost, Or the Spiritual Drifter as Poet." Reprinted from *The Function of Criticism*, Denver: Swallow, 1957, pp. 159-187. Reprinted by permission of the publisher, Alan Swallow. Copyright 1957 by Yvor Winters.

but this is merely another way of saying that the reader feels a kinship to him and likes him easily. Classical literature is said to judge human experience with respect to the norm; but it does so with re- [159] spect to the norm of what humanity ought to be, not with respect to the norm of what it happens to be in a particular place and time. The human average has never been admirable, and in certain cultures it has departed very far from the admirable; that is why in the great classical periods of literature we are likely to observe great works in tragedy and satire, the works of a Racine and a Molière, of a Shakespeare and a Jonson, works which deal in their respective ways with sharp deviations from the ideal norm; and that is why literature which glorifies the average is sentimental rather than classical.

Frost writes of rural subjects, and the American reader of our time has an affection for rural subjects which is partly the product of the Romantic sentimentalization of "nature," but which predominated in this nation a generation or two ago; the rural life is somehow regarded as the truly American life. I have no objection to the poet's employing rural settings; but we should remember that it is the poet's business to evaluate human experience, and the rural setting is no more valuable for this purpose than any other or than no particular setting, and one could argue with some plausibility that an exclusive concentration on it may be limiting.

Frost early began his endeavor to make his style approximate as closely as possible the style of conversation, and this endeavor has added to his reputation: it has helped to make him seem "natural." But poetry is not conversation, and I see no reason why poetry should be called upon to imitate conversation. Conversation is the most careless and formless of human utterance; it is spontaneous and unrevised, and its vocabulary is commonly limited. Poetry is the most difficult form of human utterance; we revise poems carefully in order to make them more nearly perfect. The two forms of expression are extremes, they are not close to each other. We do not praise a violinist for playing as if he were improvising; we praise him for playing well. And when a man plays well or writes well, his audience must have intelligence, training, and patience in order to appreciate him. We do not understand difficult matters "naturally."

The business of the poet can be stated simply. The poet deals

136

[160] with human experience in words. Words are symbols of concepts, which have acquired connotation of feeling in addition to their denotation of concept. The poet, then, as a result of the very nature of his medium, must make a rational statement about an experience, and as rationality is a part of the medium, the ultimate value of the poem will depend in a fair measure on the soundness of the rationality: it is possible, of course, to reason badly, just as it is possible to reason well. But the poet is deliberately employing the connotative content of language as well as the denotative; so that what he must do is make a rational statement about an experience, at the same time employing his language in such a manner as to communicate the emotion which ought to be communicated by that rational understanding of the particular subject. In so far as he is able to do this, the poem will be good; in so far as the subject itself is important, the poem will be great. That is, a poem which merely describes a stone may be excellent but will certainly be minor; whereas a poem which deals with man's contemplation of death and eternity, or with a formative decision of some kind may be great. It is possible, of course, that the stone may be treated in such a way that it symbolizes something greater than itself; but if this occurs, the poem is about something greater than the stone. The poet is valuable, therefore, in proportion to his ability to apprehend certain kinds of objective truth; in proportion as he is great, he will not resemble ourselves but will resemble what we ought to be. It becomes our business, then, to endeavor to resemble him, and this endeavor is not easy and for this reason few persons make it. Country conversation and colloquial charm are irrelevant to the real issue. The great poets, men like Ben Jonson and Fulke Greville, have few readers; though some of them, like Milton, are widely admired from a distance. But they offer us, in their best efforts, the finest understanding of human experience to which we have access; some people are able and willing to understand them, and the human intelligence, however precariously, is thus kept alive. If we set up false ideals of human nature, and our best poets judge experience in terms of them and so beguile us into doing likewise, the human intelligence is to that extent diminished. [161]

Frost has said that Emerson is his favorite American poet, and he himself appears to be something of an Emersonian. Emerson was a Romantic pantheist: he identified God with the universe; he taught that impulse comes directly from God and should be obeyed, that through surrender to impulse we become one with God; he taught that reason is man-made and bungling and should be suppressed. In moral and aesthetic doctrine, Emerson was a relativist; his most thorough-going disciples in American literature were Walt Whitman and Hart Crane. In Frost, on the other hand, we find a disciple without Emerson's religious conviction: Frost believes in the rightness of impulse, but does not discuss the pantheistic doctrine which would give authority to impulse; as a result of his belief in impulse, he is of necessity a relativist, but his relativism, apparently since it derives from no intense religious conviction, has resulted mainly in ill-natured eccentricity and in increasing melancholy. He is an Emersonian who has become sceptical and uncertain without having reformed; and the scepticism and uncertainty do not appear to have been so much the result of thought as the result of the impact upon his sensibility of conflicting notions of his own era—they appear to be the result of his having taken the easy way and having drifted with the various currents of his time. [162]

ꙮ REGINALD L. COOK[11]

Unlike Walt Whitman, Frost does not hook you round the waist with his left arm while his right hand points to continental landscapes or the varied vistas of the public roads. Frost's elbows do not rest in sea-gaps; his palms do not cover continents. Nor does he fly the flights of a fluid and swallowing soul. Whitman's identification with the multi-dimensional world appears exaggerated and self-intoxicated beside Frost's self-restricted actualism. Neither does he, like Emerson, shadow-box with big, bland, transcendental abstractions. Of late, he is like one who, ascending foothills, looks toward higher and further ranges of the [101] mind and spirit. A kneeler at well-curbs, a stargazer, a fatigued apple-picker, a leaf-treader, it never has been his intent to tran-

---

[11] From *The Dimensions of Robert Frost*, New York: Rinehart, 1958, pp. 101-103.

scend the finite or the specific, the concrete or the common. He is sufficiently satisfied in "setting the thing that is supreme."

His literalness is an asset because it makes cherishable what lies in the line of vision. Doubtless, he would agree with Thoreau that "a true account of the actual is the purest poetry," but he would emphasize the "true account," which would mean to him neither photographic description nor idealized action. He distinguishes between the realist who likes his potato with the dirt on it and the one who likes the potato brushed clean. He believes that "the thing that art does for life is to clean it, to strip it to form." He says:

> Let chaos storm!
> Let cloud shapes swarm!
> I wait for form.

Possessing a classicist's devotion to form and a realist's interest in the quality of life inhering in concrete experience, his observing eye selects facts common in experience. By making the facts yield their essence, he eludes their domination, and this is why, for him, the fact is not the most imperious, but rather "the sweetest dream that labor knows." He would not agree with Wordsworth's "Peter Bell":

> A primrose by a river's brim
> A yellow primrose was to him,
> And it was nothing more.

Peter Bell's perception of the primrose is retinal. Frost grasps the particular fact in an effort to suggest the universal to which it is related as the part is related to the whole. To quote Wordsworth again, Frost is one

> Who looks
> In steadiness, who hath among least things
> An undersense of the greatest; sees the parts
> As parts, but with a feeling of the whole.

He knows that by refining a thought to its essentials you multiply the levels of meaning. [102]

Recognizing the importance of the realistic fact tethered in human experience, he has never abandoned himself to the romantic dream of a "wild dedication of yourself/To unpath'd waters, undreamed shores." Poe's heart-wrenching questioning of science:

Hast thou not torn the Naiad from her flood,
The Elfin from the green grass, and from me
The summer dream beneath the tamarind tree?

is the antithesis of Frost's assertion that "the sweetest dream"
that labor knows is what "the fact" suggests. Frost gives us the
fact *plus* its overtone, presented without undue strain. In "The
Armful" we gather by implication he is an equilibrist, a balancer:
one who takes time out to stack his armful of "extremes too hard
to comprehend at once" in a better load. The poem accurately
describes an intimate experience, and it implies more than the
actual fact. In "The Tuft of Flowers," he not only presents a
little pastoral scene, but he also suggests man's alliance with others
in co-operative enterprise. A butterfly draws the eye of a solitary
haymaker to "a leaping tongue of bloom" beside a reedy brook,
in consequence of which he feels a sensibility kindred to his
own in the mower who spared the tuft of flowers. The poet says:

"Men work together," I told him from the heart,
"Whether they work together or apart."

This is the overtone which the fact suggests, the intimation that
the experience evokes.

In "Leaves Compared with Flowers" he says:

Leaves and bark, leaves and bark,
To lean against and hear in the dark.
Petals I may have once pursued.
Leaves are all my darker mood.

"Leaves are all my darker mood," he tells us. The smoothness
of the leaves and the roughness of the bark have a special significance for him. Ardent desires of earlier years give way before
sober and enduring satisfactions. Here again the common fact
suggests the overtone. [103]

✿ J. DONALD ADAMS[12]

A year ago, following the presentation of the 1958 National Book Awards, I relieved my mind about a number of things: the iniquities attendant upon literary prizes, overlong speeches before captive audiences, and the discomfort which ensues when several hundred people make a simultaneous assault upon a couple of tables bearing assorted glassware and bottled goods. But chiefly, I grew hot over one of the most virulent forms of snobbery we have today—which is literary snobbery. Today I am moved to dispute—and hotly—certain statements made by Professor Lionel Trilling at the 85th birthday dinner in honor of Robert Frost.

Only last week I was writing about those writers who are indubitably American. Frost is pre-eminently of their company. That this is so, Professor Trilling did not deny, yet I suspect that Frost had difficulty in recognizing himself in the mirror which Professor Trilling held up to him, for it was badly cracked.

Professor Trilling admitted an understandable diffidence to which he gave graceful expression, for the professor has a subtle and trained intelligence, plus a gift for lucid exposition. His difficulty was that although—or perhaps I should say because—he is a native New Yorker, he showed little understanding of the United States. That circumstance has not, however, prevented other sons of this city from grasping more fully the meaning of the American experience. Professor Trilling's failure to do so is, indeed, one widely shared by other American intellectuals.

Before stating the bases for his diffidence, Professor Trilling made that obeisance to "myth" which is obligatory for critics in his camp, and hastily hunted out a symbol or two—critical occupations without which some of our quarterlies could not go to press. It was a trifle unfortunate, I think, in view of Frost's shock of white hair, that the professor should have identified the poet with the Bald Eagle—but let that pass.

Besides the natural diffidence which any speaker would have

---

[12] "Speaking of Books," *New York Times Book Review* (April 12, 1959), p. 2.

felt upon this occasion, Professor Trilling named several others. He could not help knowing, he said, that "the manifest America of Robert Frost's poems is not the America that has its place in my own mind"—Frost's manifest America being rural, and his urban. Then, he said, he had for a long time been alienated from Frost's work "by what I saw in it that either itself seemed to denigrate the work of the critical intellect" (an urban faculty, in the professor's estimation) "or that gave its admirers the ground for making the denigration."

Presently Professor Trilling made it clear that *his* Frost "is not the Frost I seem to perceive existing in the minds of so many of his admirers. He is not the Frost that confounds the characteristically modern practice of poetry by his notable democratic simplicity of utterance: on the contrary. He is not the Frost who controverts the bitter modern astonishment at the nature of human life: the opposite is so. He is not the Frost who reassures us by his affirmation of old virtues, simplicities, pieties, and ways of feeling: anything but."

Professor Trilling found his key to the understanding of his Frost in D. H. Lawrence's criticism of American literature; if he had re-read, or read, Emerson instead, he might have lost *his* Frost and discovered the one he turns his back on, for a goodly part of Frost the man and Frost the poet is rooted, deeply rooted, in Emerson, who was his intellectual and spiritual godfather. Lawrence had some perceptive things to say about American writers, but he failed in ultimate understanding of them, and of the American experience. Like Professor Trilling himself, he was too lost in the Freudian wood; Lawrence was no Daniel Boone. We did not need Lawrence to tell us that the great writers of the classic tradition were radicals; any thoughtful American boy of sixteen, encountering Emerson and Thoreau, has his world turned topsy-turvy, and I wish our pap-fed adolescents read them now. If they did, our future would look a lot brighter than it does.

Professor Trilling confessed that he thinks of Frost as a "terrifying" poet, and that "the universe he conceives is a terrifying universe." Holy mackerel! Frost simply sees the universe as it is and accepts it. He isn't terrified by what he sees, and neither should we be. He takes it in his stride, which is one reason why he is in there pitching at 85; he has a private air-conditioning system denied to most of his younger contemporaries—and, as I said before, he got it from Emerson.

Come out of the Freudian wood, Professor Trilling, and face the facts of life. Don't take Lawrence so seriously; he was a gifted but terribly confused man, as you and most of us at this present moment, are. All this country needs is to recapture its earlier vision. One of the silliest remarks ever made about the American experience came from one of the editors of your favorite magazine, the *Partisan Review*. Mr. William Phillips solemnly observed that American literature has played hide-and-seek with American experience for lack of "an image, or cluster of images, of the national experience available to literature." No such lack exists, and both of you should re-read one of the great American poems. It is by Robert Frost, and it is called "The Gift Outright."
[2]

✴ M. L. ROSENTHAL[13]

I don't know just what Lionel Trilling said at Robert Frost's eighty-fifth birthday party; I gather he pointed out, with heart-stirring allusions to Sophocles and the whole tradition of tragic poetry, the obvious fact that Frost has dark depths which make him something more than a rural Longfellow. Whatever he said, it shivered J. Donald Adams' frail, sagging timbers something awful. With the irritation of any man startled out of a deep sleep, Adams wrote a furious column in *The New York Times*. Those New York intellectuals, he cried, don't know the real, rural America; they should read more Emerson and less Lawrence; they're "lost in the Freudian woods." Other Furies flew into the *Times* letter-column to say it was high time those Trilling-types were shot in their tracks. But in all this glorious firing of popguns, I love best Mr. Adams' fit of abysmal indignation:

Professor Trilling confessed that he thinks of Frost as a "terrifying" poet, and that "the universe he conceives is a terrifying

[13] "The Robert Frost Controversy," *Nation*, CLXXXVIII (June 20, 1959), 559-561.

universe." Holy mackerel! Frost simply sees the universe as it is and accepts it. . . .

I can't decide whether I prefer the "Holy mackerel!" or the "simply"—or the bland assumption that Frost is an indigenous poet who rose into prominence as naturally and easily as your Aunt Sally learnt how to bake those blueberry pies for which our boys fought and died. Frost had to move to England when he was thirty-seven, and assimilate himself to the Georgian movement there, before he could get any recognition at all. As Pound put it more than twenty years ago, speaking of the inability of the J. Donald Adamses to recognize the real thing right under their noses, "Even Frost the prize autochthonous specimen made his début in London, and was forced into the local New England bucolic recognition from Kensington, W. 8. The *pièces justificatives* are the back files of *Poetry* and the *Egoist* from October 1912 onward. The *Little Review*, 1917-19, as monthly, with the later quarterly issues." And two decades before *this*, reviewing *North of Boston* (published by David Nutt in England in 1914), Pound asked: "Why, IF there are serious people in America, desiring literature of America, literature accepting present conditions, rendering American life with sober fidelity—why, in heaven's name, is this book of New England Eclogues given under a foreign imprint?"

All of which goes to show, "simply," [559] that it took the foreigners, the expatriates, and the new critics they sparked into action to push this spokesman for one kind of American experience into indifferent American faces. Once he broke through the barrier, however, the publicists (with the aid of Frost's own public personality) turned him into the sagacious and humorous country-poet Mr. Adams loves. This role is one variant of that grand archetype the Good Grey Poet into which they have relegated Whitman and Sandburg; one would never guess the brute realities Frost so often deals with. Frost himself, as it happens, does not encourage people to think about them, and perhaps has half-forgotten his own horror at some of his realizations. It is easier for the general reader, and for the poet as a popular figure, to think of his work as a kind of rich radiation outwards from a basic foundation of nature-poetry and local-colorism. Certainly the wonderful specificity of his impressions of persons

144

and places and experiences is inseparable from the fabric of almost any Frost-poem.

> These flowery waters and these watery flowers
> From snow that melted only yesterday.
> —"Spring Pools."

> I'm going out to clean the pasture spring;
> I'll only stop to rake the leaves away
> (And wait to watch the water clear, I may) . . .
> —"The Pasture"

> Out in the ploughed ground in the cold a digger,
> Among unearthed potatoes standing still,
> Was counting winter dinners, one a hill. . . .
> —"The Investment"

This is the deceptive staple of Frost's reputation, this lyrical and realistic repossession of the rural and the "natural." For most of his readers it has the charm of the completely exotic; literate America is not, for the most part, to be found in "the country," and moreover the world of modern poetry has been dominated by a metropolitan consciousness. Frost gives us welcome release from that consciousness, puts us in touch with something "purer," something idyllic, which yet is miraculously real. The "digger" and his wife in "The Investment" are even miserably poor, though not defeated by their poverty. But beyond the surface appeal of all this, there lurks the further implication of the "terrifying" which Trilling feels and every other perceptive reader must feel. At his most intense Frost is as close to the panicky edge of sensibility as Eliot. The kind of mind at work in his poetry is neither that of a plain New England farmer nor that of a Romantic rediscoverer of the land. It is what Yeats called "the modern mind in search of its own meanings." The spirit is comparable to that of the English Georgians among whom Frost first became certain of his true bearings. Only, his work is richer than theirs in every way; it includes the nostalgic, it "proves" the pastoral pleasures, it savors the contemplative calm ancient poets praised, but it also seeks to encompass the dreadful and the neurasthenia-breeding aspects of man's existence as the modern consciousness feels them.

Nothing quite brings out Frost's "morbidity" so painfully as his poems centering on the characters of women. The wife's hysteria in "Home Burial" is a characteristic outlet for this poet's shocked sense of the helpless cruelty of things. Set against the husband's accursed matter-of-factness (not that *he* lacks feeling either), it provides the decisive energy of the poem. The woman's voice carries the pain of a primal wound:

> If you had any feelings, you that dug
> With your own hand—how could you?—his little grave;
> I saw you from that very window there,
> Making the gravel leap and leap in air,
> Leap up, like that, like that, and land so lightly
> And roll back down the mound beside the hole. . . .

Frost's men, with some exceptions, play the game more according to the rules. They take pride in their workmanship, as does the poor home-burier, and thereby can hold life's destructive terrors at bay. Perhaps something of this sort is implied (in addition to a plea of guilt at remaining aloof from struggles involving "the common good") in the confessional stanza of "Two Tramps in Mud Time":

> Good blocks of oak it was I split. . . .
> The blows that a life of self-control
> Spares to strike for the common good
> That day, giving a loose to my soul,
> I spent on the unimportant wood.

The women, however, are likely to be overborne by an ultimate emptiness or grossness or fear. In the speaker's own *persona* or that of some other male figure, we find almost always some saving humor or sense of valued mystery or deliberate understatement. Not so in female-dominated poems like "The Hill Wife," "A Servant to Servants" and "The Subverted Flower." This last poem gives the character of a young girl a surprising turn; she is subtly pictured as both innocent and mean and narrow, and the interest of this characterization is such that we are almost diverted from the glimpse of sexual squalor she has shared with her shamefaced would-be lover. The abyss yawns in this poem, whose mixture of disgust and naked terror is like the death-horror of the first stanza of "Design." Both poems portray the perversion of vital force implicit in the very structure of existence. In "Design" the effect of *morbidezza* comes from the awful, silent whiteness, the grotesque acrobatics of the little circus-act Frost says he has come upon.

> I found a dimpled spider, fat and white,
> On a white heal-all, holding up a moth
> Like a white piece of rigid satin cloth—
> Assorted characters of death and blight
> Mixed ready to begin the morning right,
> Like the ingredients of a witches' broth—
> A snow-drop spider, a flower like a froth,
> And dead wings carried like a paper kite.

The sestet of this sonnet lapses into a tiresomely "profound" questioning reminiscent of Hardy and Robinson, its point being to find in this uniquely dreadful configuration some "purpose"—

> What but design of darkness to appall?—
> If design govern in a thing so small.

What oft was thought and oft so well expressed—and that brings us to another subject. Frost *has* his weaknesses (sententiousness and a certain formal timidity), and I think the poetic community is on the whole aware of them. At his frequent best he dams them off or washes them out entirely. Who thinks of them in the midst of the bizarre, soul-chilling characterizations of "The Pauper Witch of Grafton" and "The Witch of Coös," or in the face of a dazzling line like

> Ten million silver lizards out of snow!

But they are there, and he has a [560] right to them, as it were. No man—especially a man whose true virtues are as compelling as Frost's—was ever made an inch taller by false praise. The real poet is engaged, to echo Yeats again, in a quarrel with himself. It is never a case of his being either a great, sunny genius of The Folk or nothing. Frost is much more than his weaknesses, but without them I do not think his strengths would be what they are. Something there is in him that does not love a pure, simple, extroverted affirmation, and the special character of his work rises from his resisting the temptation to betray his own nature. That struggle is very American—also very European, human, Emersonian, Freudian, or what have you—and he wages it even in his lesser moments, as in the couplet ending "Design" or in the

147

(to my mind) overrated "The Gift Outright," which Mr. Adams praises because of what he doubtless imagines its unqualified nativism of feeling. It is a powerful native voice Frost brings to us, idiosyncratic and stubborn—no doubt of that. But it has not yet really been listened to after all, despite all the copies of *Collected Poems* printed and sold in the last three decades. [561]

❧ LIONEL TRILLING[14]

On March 26th, Henry Holt and Company, the publishers of Robert Frost, gave Mr. Frost a dinner at the Waldorf-Astoria in celebration of his eighty-fifth birthday. I was the speaker at the dinner. I am publishing what I said about Mr. Frost not because I think it to be especially interesting in itself but because it made the occasion for a disturbance of some magnitude and I should like to answer the question that has often been put to me: What did I say that could so nearly have approached a scandal?

Some of the substance of my speech was made public by J. Donald Adams in his column in *The New York Times Book Review* of April 12th. Mr. Adams wrote from a copy of my manuscript which, with my permission, had been made available to him by Henry Holt and Company, and he reported with sufficient accuracy those parts of the speech to which he took exception. It should be said of Mr. Adams's reply to me that it took exception only to the critical judgment I had expressed. Mr. Adams did not question my taste or tact except in one small and perhaps facetious instance—he thought it "unfortunate . . . in view of Frost's shock of white hair," that I should have "identified the poet with the Bald Eagle." (But every American worthy of the name knows that the Bald Eagle is not bald at all and that in maturity it is distinguished by its shock of white hair.) Nevertheless the reply of Mr. Adams created the impression with some people that, so far from my having paid tribute to a venerable man at a celebration of his life and achievement, I had actually offered him an affront. I gather that the chief cause of

---

[14] "A Speech on Robert Frost: A Cultural Episode," *Partisan Review*, XXVI (Summer 1959), 445-452. By permission of the author.

the presumed offense was my having spoken of Mr. Frost as "a terrifying poet."

Certainly what I had said as reported by Mr. Adams offered an affront to some part of American opinion. It was a very deep affront if I can judge by the letters, published in the *Book Review* [445] of April 26th, which applauded Mr. Adams for his reply to me. There were nine such letters and all of them sounded a note of bitterness, or of personal grievance, or of triumph over my having been so thoroughly taken down by Mr. Adams. I must confess to being surprised by the low personal and intellectual tone of these letters. My estimate of the present state of American culture had not prepared me for it. "Trilling doesn't have the good sense to know when he is out of his field or his depth or whatever it is." "Frost might have had the Nobel Prize if so many New York critics hadn't gone whoring after European gods." "This Trilling fella had it coming to him for some time." "I hope Robert Frost was having a nice plate of buckwheat cakes and Vermont maple syrup as he read Mr. Adams's remarks. He couldn't have done better unless he had taken the so-called professor out to the woodshed." "I am a Freudian psychoanalyst, but I couldn't agree with Mr. Adams more. Imagine calling Frost a 'terrifying poet.' Professor Trilling never got lost in the Freudian wood. He is just enmeshed in a Trilling world." (In his column Mr. Adams had urged me "to come out of the Freudian wood . . . and face the facts of life." It will be seen that I make no mention of Freud in my speech, but I do speak of D. H. Lawrence, and Mr. Adams said that Lawrence was a genius but hadn't understood "the American experience" because, like me, he was "lost in the Freudian wood." Lawrence, of course, hated Freud and took every occasion to denounce him.)

The personal and intellectual quality of the letters is especially interesting because of the professions of the people who wrote them: in addition to the "Freudian psychoanalyst," the writers included the editor of *The Atlantic Monthly*, the publisher of *The Saturday Review*, two fairly well-known poets, a member of the Federal Trade Commission, a well-known and quite literate writer of fiction and biography, a very distinguished literary scholar. Only one of the writers, Mr. Weeks of *The Atlantic Monthly*, knew at first hand, what I had said, having been present at the dinner. He expressed himself as finding my remarks "ill-judged and condescending for an occasion which was intended to be appreciative," and went on to say that "it would have been more appropriate had the introduction been entrusted to W. H. Auden, particularly in view of England's early acceptance of Frost's work, in which case we should have been spared the long Freudian self-analysis which few could have come to hear." All the other writers knew what I had said only from Mr. Adams's reply to it. That the literary scholar was among their number made a circumstance to which I couldn't fail to respond with some un- [446] happiness, for I had first been Professor Emery Neff's student when I was an undergraduate at Columbia College and I had worked in his field and under his direction as a graduate student; I have always thought of Mr. Neff as the teacher from whom I had learned the methods and attitudes of the scholar; that he should so far have abrogated the rule and spirit of scholarship as to write in support of Mr. Adams's rebuke (as he chose to call it) without having seen the text of what I had said disturbed me deeply in a way I shall not now attempt to describe.

I have no doubt that the episode will yield cultural conclusions to whoever wants to draw them.

Because I am publishing the speech as a document, I give it exactly as I spoke it, not even mitigating the donnish humor of the opening paragraphs.

* * *

Mr. Rigg, Ladies and Gentlemen
(and I shall address Mr. Frost presently):

I am sure that anyone standing in my place to-night, charged with the happy office of greeting Mr. Frost on his birthday, on his massive, his Sophoclean birthday, would be bound to feel, as I do indeed feel, a considerable measure of diffidence.

For our occasion, although it isn't solemn, is surely momentous. We all of us know that we celebrate something that lies beyond even Mr. Frost's achievement as a poet. No person here tonight, no matter how high his regard for Mr. Frost as a poet may be, is under any illusion that Mr. Frost, at this point in his career, exists in the consciousness of Americans as only a poet. Just what he does exist as may perhaps be best understood by the archaeologists of a few millenniums hence. They will observe, those ardent students of our culture, how, at the time of the vernal equinox, feasts were held to celebrate the birth of this personage, and how, at a later time in the spring, at that ceremony which the ancient North Americans, with their infallible instinct for beauty, called by the lovely name of *Commencement*, it was customary to do him honor by a rite in which it was pretended that he was a scholar, a man of immense learning—a doctor—and no American university was thought to be worthy of the name until it had duly performed this rite, which was quaintly called *conferring a degree*. The time of year at which these ritual observances took place makes it plain to the archaeologists that they are almost certainly not dealing with an historical individual but [447] rather with a solar myth, a fertility figure. They go on to expound the subtle process of myth which is to be observed in the fact that this vernal spirit was called *Frost*, a name which seems to contradict his nature and function. In their effort to explain this anomaly, they take note of evidence which suggests that the early North Americans believed that there were once two brothers, Robert Frost and Jack Frost, of whom one, Jack, remained unregenerate and hostile to mankind, while the other brother became its friend. But of course the archaeologists understand that this is a mere folk-explanation which explains nothing. They say, cogently enough, that mythical figures often embody contradictory principles, that just as Apollo was both destroyer and preserver, so Robert Frost was at one and the same time both ice and sun, and they point to a dark saying attributed to him: "Like a piece of ice on a hot stove, the poem must ride on its own melting."

Thus the ultimate myth. It tells us much about the nature of Robert Frost and I am glad to be able to communicate it to you.

But there is also the myth that is nearer at hand. We do not need to wait upon the archaeologists of the future to understand that Robert Frost exists not only in a human way but also in a mythical way. We know him, and have known him so for many years, as nothing less than a national fact. We have come to think of him as virtually a symbol of America, as something not unlike an articulate, an actually poetic, Bald Eagle. When we undertake to honor him, we do indeed honor him as a poet, but also as a tutelary genius of the nation and as a justification of our national soul.

This mythical existence of Robert Frost determines the nature of our occasion and makes it momentous. It substantiates my statement that anyone who speaks publicly about Mr. Frost tonight must do so under the constraints of an extreme diffidence.

Yet I must be more weighed down by diffidence than many others who might speak here. I must almost entertain a doubt of the appropriateness of my speaking here at all. For I cannot help knowing that the manifest America of Robert Frost's poems is not the America that has its place in my own mind. The manifest America of Mr. Frost's poems is rural, and, if I may say so, it is rural in a highly moralized way, in an aggressively moralized way. It thus represents an ideal that is common to many Americans, perhaps especially to Americans of the literary kind, who thus express their distaste [448] for the life of the city and for all that the city implies of excessive complexity, of uncertainty, of anxiety, and of the demand that is made upon intellect to deal with whatever are the causes of complexity, uncertainty, anxiety.

I do not share this ideal. It is true that the image of the old America has a great power over me—that old America with which the America of Mr. Frost's poems seems to be continuous. And I think I know from experience—there are few Americans who do not—how intense can be the pleasure in the hills and the snow, in the meadows and woods and swamps that make the landscape of Mr. Frost's manifest America; and know, too, how great a part this pleasure can play in a man's moral being. But these natural things that give me pleasure constitute my notion of the earthly paradise, they are not the ruling elements of my imagination of actual life. Those elements are urban—I speak here tonight incongruously as a man of the city. I teach in an urban university. The magazine I most enjoy writing for is *Partisan Review*, to which, as I know, there is often imputed an excess of city intellectuality, even to the point of its being thought scarcely American at all.

Of course I have imagination enough to hate the city. And of course I have sensibility enough to be bored and exasperated by the intellectual life that is peculiar to the city, not only as that is lived by others but by myself. But to the essential work that is done by the critical intellect (I use the term in its widest sense), that work which, wherever it is carried on, must sooner or later relate itself to the metropolis or must seek, wherever it is carried on, to create around itself the intensity and variety that traditionally characterize the intellectual life of the metropolis—to that work I give a partisan devotion. I know all that can be charged against the restless, combative, abstract urban intellect: I know perhaps more than is known by its avowed antagonists. I also know that when it flags, something goes out of the nation's spirit, and that if it were to cease, the state of the nation would be much the worse.

It is a fact which I had best confess as simply as possible that for a long time I was alienated from Mr. Frost's great canon of work by what I saw in it, that either itself seemed to denigrate the work of the critical intellect or that gave to its admirers the ground for making the denigration. It was but recently that my resistance, at the behest of better understanding, yielded to admiration—it is [449] probable that there is no one here to-night who has not admired Mr. Frost's poetry for a longer time than I have.

This will begin to explain why I am so especially diffident standing in this place. I have yet more to confess. I have to say that my Frost—*my Frost:* what airs we give ourselves when once we believe that we have come into possession of a poet!—I have to say that my Frost is not the Frost I seem to perceive existing in the minds of so many of his admirers. He is not the Frost who confounds the characteristically modern practice of poetry by his notable democratic simplicity of utterance: on the contrary. He is not the Frost who controverts the bitter modern astonishment at the nature of human life: the opposite is so. He is not the Frost who reassures us by his affirmation of old virtues, simplicities, pieties, and ways of feeling: anything but. I will not go so far as to say that my Frost is not essentially an American poet at all: I believe that he is quite as American as everyone thinks he is, but not in the way that everyone thinks he is.

In the matter of the Americanism of American literature one of my chief guides is that very remarkable critic, D. H. Lawrence. Here are the opening sentences of Lawrence's great outrageous book about classic American literature. "We like to think of the old fashioned American classics as children's books. Just childishness on our part. The old American art speech contains an alien quality which belongs to the American continent and to nowhere else." And this unique alien quality, Lawrence goes on to say, the

153

world has missed. "It is hard to hear a new voice," he says, "as hard as to listen to an unknown language. . . . Why? Out of fear. The world fears a new experience more than it fears anything. It can pigeonhole any idea. But it can't pigeonhole a real new experience. It can only dodge. The world is a great dodger, and the Americans the greatest. Because they dodge their own very selves." I should like to pick up a few more of Lawrence's sentences, feeling the freer to do so because they have an affinity to Mr. Frost's prose manner and substance: "An artist is usually a damned liar, but his art, if it be art, will tell you the truth of his day. And that is all that matters. Away with eternal truth. Truth lives from day to day. . . . The old American artists were hopeless liars. . . . Never trust the artist. Trust the tale. The proper function of the critic is to save the tale from the artist who created it. . . . Now listen to me, don't listen to him. He'll tell you the lie you expect, which is partly your fault for expecting it." [450]

Now in point of fact Robert Frost is *not* a liar. I would not hesitate to say that he was if I thought he was. But no, he is not. In certain of his poems—I shall mention one or two in a moment —he makes it perfectly plain what he is doing; and if we are not aware of what he is doing in other of his poems, where he is not quite so plain, that is not his fault but our own. It is not from him that the tale needs to be saved.

I conceive that Robert Frost is doing in his poems what Lawrence says the great writers of the classic American tradition did. That enterprise of theirs was of an ultimate radicalism. It consisted, Lawrence says, of two things: a disintegration and sloughing off of the old consciousness, by which Lawrence means the old European consciousness, and the forming of a new consciousness underneath.

So radical a work, I need scarcely say, is not carried out by reassurance, nor by the affirmation of old virtues and pieties. It is carried out by the representation of the terrible actualities of life in a new way. I think of Robert Frost as a terrifying poet. Call him, if it makes things any easier, a tragic poet, but it might be useful every now and then to come out from under the shelter of that literary word. The universe that he conceives is a terrifying universe. Read the poem called "Design" and see if you sleep the better for it. Read "Neither Out Far Nor In Deep," which often seems to me the most perfect poem of our time, and see if you are warmed by anything in it except the energy with which emptiness is perceived.

But the *people*, it will be objected, the *people* who inhabit this possibly terrifying universe! About them there is nothing that can terrify; surely the people in Mr. Frost's poems can only reassure us by their integrity and solidity. Perhaps so. But I cannot make the disjunction. It may well be that ultimately they reassure us in some sense, but first they terrify us, or should. We must not be misled about them by the curious tenderness with which they are represented, a tenderness which extends to a recognition of the tenderness which they themselves can often give. But when ever have people been so isolated, so lightning-blasted, so tried down and calcined by life, so reduced, each in his own way, to some last irreducible core of being. Talk of the disintegration and sloughing off of the old consciousness! The people of Robert Frost's poems have done that with a vengeance. Lawrence says that what the Americans refused to accept was "the post-Renaissance humanism of Europe," "the old Euro- [451] pean spontaneity," "the flowing easy humor of Europe" and that seems to me a good way to describe the people who inhabit Robert Frost's America. In the interests of what great other thing these people have made this rejection we cannot know for certain. But we can guess that it was in the interest of truth, of some truth of the self. This is what they all affirm by their humor (which is so *not* "the easy flowing humor of Europe"), by their irony, by their separateness and isolateness. They affirm *this* of themselves: that they are what they are, that this is their truth, and that if the truth be bare, as truth often is, it is far better than a lie. For me the process by which they arrive at that truth is always terrifying. The manifest America of Mr. Frost's poems may be pastoral; the actual America is tragic.

And what new consciousness is forming underneath? That I do not know, possibly because I have not been long enough habituated to the voice that makes the relatively new experience I am having. I am still preoccupied with the terrifying process of the disintegration and sloughing off of the old consciousness.

Mr. Frost:

I hope that you will not think it graceless of me that on your birthday I have undertaken to say that a great many of your admirers have not understood clearly what you have been doing in your life in poetry. I know that you will not say which of us is in the right of the matter. You will behave like the Secret whose conduct you have described:

> We dance around in a ring and suppose.
> But the Secret sits in the middle and knows.

And I hope that you will not think it graceless of me that on your birthday I have made you out to be a poet who terrifies. When I began to speak I called your birthday Sophoclean and that word has, I think, controlled everything I have said about you. Like you, Sophocles lived to a great age, writing well; and like you, Sophocles was the poet his people loved most. Surely they loved him in some part because he praised their common country. But I think that they loved him chiefly because he made plain to them the terrible things of human life: they felt, perhaps, that only a poet who could make plain the terrible things could possibly give them comfort. [452]

❦ ROBERT LANGBAUM[15]

What has happened to nature poetry? Ask this question of your up-to-date kind of poetry reader, and you will get a stare of blank amazement. There isn't any, he will mutter, although he will soon concede that there *is* Robert Frost. If he admires Frost, he will probably assure you that Frost is no mere nature poet, the implication being that nature poetry can no longer have serious relevance. He will have behind him the authority of critical opinion, of even Joseph Warren Beach, who, in *The Concept of Nature in Nineteenth-Century English Poetry*, the most thorough study of the subject, says that the very name and concept of nature have virtually disappeared from twentieth-

15 From "The New Nature Poetry." Reprinted from *American Scholar*, XXVIII (Summer 1959), 323-340. Copyright 1960 by United Chapters of Phi Beta Kappa. By permission of the publishers.

century poetry. Frost himself is not a nature poet, says Beach, since he writes not about nature but about this, that and the other thing in the country.

Beach has in mind the philosophical and protoreligious concept of nature that flourished in the eighteenth century and was already on its way out in the nineteenth. The religion of nature derived from Newton's demonstration that everything from the fall of an apple to the movement of planets is governed by a single law. To people whose Christianity was waning, a nature so orderly seemed to offer new evidence of God's existence and a new source of religious emotion. But the religion of nature was threatened, first, by early nineteenth-century geology, which found in the rocks evidence of catastrophes that had wiped out whole species, and finally by Darwin's theory that the evolution of species is governed by a mindless force called natural selection. Under these assaults, nature poetry declined. Swinburne tried to be optimistic about post-Darwinian nature, and Hardy was definitely pessimistic about it. But [323] both were being anthropomorphic still, at a time when the exciting new concept, the only one that could inspire conviction, was that of the mindlessness of nature, its nonhuman otherness: a concept having nothing to do with optimism or pessimism.

Now it is just this sense of nature that a number of contemporary American poets render superbly; so that far from being extinct, nature poetry has enjoyed a revival. It is better than it has been in a long time. . . . But why, if this poetry is so good, should it be necessary to point out its existence? Because, I think, the term *nature poetry* has fallen into such disrepute that no one wants to apply it to poems he likes; and because critics who are looking for the eighteenth-century concept of nature will not find it in poems that are precisely trying to rescue nature, as it is in itself, from the outmoded concept. [324]

In the middle of the last century, Ruskin coined the phrase, "pathetic fallacy," which defines among other things the modern reaction against the eighteenth-century style of nature poetry. The pathetic fallacy is the false description that occurs when, under the pressure of strong emotion, the poet projects human feelings into natural objects (Kingsley's "cruel, crawling foam"). Ruskin considers the pathetic fallacy justified as long as the distortion is psychologically valid, appropriate to the observer's emotion. Such poetry, in which the emotions are "strong enough to vanquish, partly, the intellect, and make it believe what they choose," can be good poetry of the second order. But in poetry of the first order, like Dante's, "the intellect also rises, till it is strong enough to assert its rule against, or together with, the utmost efforts of the [325] passions; and the whole man stands in an iron glow, white hot, perhaps, but still strong, and in no wise evaporating." Poetry of the first order retains the "plain and leafy fact" of the primrose, "whatever and how many soever the associations and passions may be that crowd around it." Not only does Ruskin anticipate Eliot's attack on the "dissociation of sensibility" from thought, but he sets forth the program of the best twentieth-century nature poetry, which defines itself precisely by opposing the pathetic fallacy.

That . . . is the point of Frost's poem, "The Need of Being Versed in Country Things," about a burnt-down farmhouse. The birds fly in and out of the abandoned barn, "Their murmur more like the sigh we sigh/From too much dwelling on what has been," but their sympathetic response is illusory. "Yet for them the lilac renewed its leaf," we are told,

> For them there was really nothing sad.
> But though they rejoiced in the nest they kept,
> One had to be versed in country things
> Not to believe the phoebes wept

—not to commit the pathetic fallacy. . . . In Frost the life of man weaves so inextricably in and out of nature that it always comes as a surprise to the speaker to discover that they are not identical. And the difference poses no real threat. The perception of it is simply salutary. This makes Frost less radically twentieth-century in his sense of nature than [Wallace] Stevens and Marianne Moore.

The difference in Frost often defines itself against such domestic considerations as that of utility and ownership. In "Going for Water," the speaker gains an insight into water not as something to be used or owned but as it is in itself; and in "The Wood-Pile," the [326] speaker realizes that the precisely cut and measured cord of firewood, unaccountably abandoned "far from a useful fireplace," has another *use:* "To warm the frozen swamp as best it could/With the slow smokeless burning of decay." There is a suggestion of danger in the famous "Stopping by Woods on a Snowy Evening," where the speaker, who has interrupted his journey homeward and trespassed on another's property to watch the woods fill up with snow, pulls himself away reluctantly:

> The woods are lovely, dark and deep,
> But I have promises to keep,
> And miles to go before I sleep,
> And miles to go before I sleep.

The momentary insight into the nonhuman otherness of nature is salutary, but to prolong it is to seek unconsciousness, individual extinction, before your time. In "Come In," the speaker, who comes at evening to the edge of a dark wood, hears thrush music inside,

> Almost like a call to come in
> To the dark and lament.
>
> But no, I was out for stars:
> I would not come in.
> I meant not even if asked,
> And I hadn't been.

To consider nature purposively dangerous is also to commit the pathetic fallacy. Besides, nature in Frost never is so dangerous that his speakers cannot protect themselves against it.

Frost takes into account nature's destructiveness, but his examples of it are seldom very frightening. The whispering scythe of "Mowing" must in performing its useful labor cut down the pale orchises and scare a bright green snake. Before they "can mount again," the leaves of "In Hardwood Groves" must "go down into the dark decayed." But the scythe is whispering in effect that all is well; while toward the natural cycle, the theme that gave birth to tragedy and religion, Frost takes a merely commonsense attitude: "However it is in some other world/I know that this is the way in ours." In "Storm Fear," the speaker, waking to hear the wind and snow seem to challenge him to come out and fight, is [327] glad not to accept the challenge and wonders in despair whether he and his family will have the strength to save themselves in the morning. But even in this poem, we know that the despair is a passing mood, that in the morning they will have the strength.

Death itself is adumbrated as a sleep in two perfect poems, "After Apple-Picking" and "An Old Man's Winter Night." In both poems, the man falls asleep when his work is almost but not quite finished, his sleep corresponds to the sleep of nature in winter, and the natural process takes over his unfinished work. Forgetting what he came to do in a roomful of barrels, the old man of the latter poem consigns to the moon his snow upon the roof, his icicles, and sleeps.

> One aged man—one man—can't keep a house,
> A farm, a countryside, or if he can,
> It's thus he does it of a winter night.

This shows harmony with nature—except that the old man's "clomping" in and out of the room makes an almost supernatural disturbance, scaring the cellar and the outer night; while the lamp he carries keeps him from seeing out-of-doors, it lights only himself with his own thoughts. The noise and the thoughts suggest the slightest disharmony with nature.

In "After Apple-Picking," it is also thoughts of the day's and season's apple-picking, of the unpicked apples and of "magnified apples" better than any on the boughs that will "trouble" the speaker's oncoming sleep, "whatever sleep it is." Is it a night's or winter's dream of the day's or autumn's activity; and is such a troubled slumber natural or supernatural?

> The woodchuck could say whether it's like his
> Long sleep, as I describe its coming on,
> Or just some human sleep.

"Just," of course, from the woodchuck's point of view, for the speculation reminds me at least of Keats's fancy that our next life will be a spiritual repetition of this one "in a finer tone."

It is not to quarrel with these poems—who could be anything but grateful for perfection?—to say that they are idyls. For there is a harmony even in the disharmony; they leave out the agony of [328] dying. Here as elsewhere Frost's acceptances are won without anguish—partly because the danger is not dangerous enough, partly because of Frost's personal strength, which is always at least equal to the danger. His darkest nature poem is

"Desert Places," where the snow and the dark wood are unambiguously desolate: "Snow falling and night falling fast, oh, fast/ . . . The woods around it have it—it is theirs."

> The loneliness includes me unawares.
>
> And lonely as it is that loneliness
> Will be more lonely ere it will be less—
> A blanker whiteness of benighted snow
> With no expression, nothing to express.
>
> They cannot scare me with their empty spaces
> Between stars—on stars where no human race is.
> I have it in me so much nearer home
> To scare myself with my own desert places.

But even here, where Frost sees nature as a void and takes into account the implications of science (rare for Frost), he turns into a kind of consolation that perception of an internal void which would be for another poet the most terrifying perception of all. "Loneliness . . . will be less" together with "scare myself" suggest that the scare is the illusory thing, almost a game (scaring one's self and others) of spooks.

Such resistance comes of sheer biological vitality, a self-preserving common sense, which Reginald Cook in a recent book on Frost calls his *sabiduria*—a Spanish word meaning "the wisdom of a people welling up in any one of its articulate members." It is *sabiduria* that keeps Frost at the edge of the "dark wood," keeps him from following his insights through to their logical implications, from risking the destructiveness of abstract thought. "The world's one globe," he says in "Build Soil,"

> human society
> Another softer globe that slightly flattened
> Rests on the world, and clinging slowly rolls.
> We have our own round shape to keep unbroken.
> The world's size has no more to do with us
> Than has the universe's. [329]

He is able to shrug off those conflicts between man and nature, thought and reality, head and heart, science and religion, which since the romantic period have torn other poets apart.

The result is a poetry that delivers us from the poignancy of the historical moment to place us in contact with a survival-making eternal folk wisdom. We can live by Frost's poetry as we could not by Yeats's or Pound's. Yet his poetry, although it must rank high in our affections, is not likely to be the favorite poetry of the most serious readers, just because Frost does not call into play all our faculties; he does not make poetry of our ideas, which in modern times have mainly to do with our sense of the age. The poets who have since the romantic period made the greatest impact are precisely those poets who have made us most aware of the historical moment, having themselves not merely known about but felt the conflicts of their age.

That is the difference between Wordsworth's nature poetry and Frost's. To talk about nature in Wordsworth's way was at the turn of the nineteenth century to be at the forefront of thought, to take into account the science, philosophy and psychology of the age, its religious skepticism, the French Revolution, the problem of the modern analytic intellect as the destroyer of feeling. If nature was orderly and the self an association of external impressions, then a life in the country would insure you the most favorable impressions. It would afford evidence of God's existence, an alternative or supplement to revolution and political reform for man's improvement, and an object that could still inspire feelings, even supernatural apprehensions. The deliberate return to nature went with the deliberate cultivation of the feelings as the necessary antidote to the conditions of modern life. No nineteenth-century reader could share in one of Wordsworth's epiphanies—one of his revelations through visible nature of "the life of things"—without a very poignant awareness of victory over the age. That is what John Stuart Mill meant when he called Wordsworth "the poet of unpoetical [distinctively modern] natures"; it is what Matthew Arnold meant when he said that in "this iron time" Wordsworth taught us to feel again.

Now Frost's sense of nature as manageable is very like [330] Wordsworth's, as is his method of conveying that sense. For Frost, too, gives us little dramatic actions that culminate in epiphanies. But Frost's are timid epiphanies, for they deliberately stop short of, where they do not explicitly repudiate, philosophical implications; and they do not arise, as they often do in Wordsworth, from an impasse in thought, thought grounded in the age. Frost's moments of awareness are accidents that could happen to any one in any age. The sign of this is that they do not change the speaker who simply goes back to his business; whereas Wordsworth's speakers undergo a measure of conversion. That is why his poems can be read in sequence as an evolution from eighteenth-century doubt through romantic transcendentalism to Christian orthodoxy.

In the sheer power to render nature, Frost may well be our best nature poet since Wordsworth. Yet it is because Frost's sense of nature is so like Wordsworth's that he does not play in our time the role Wordsworth played in his, that he leads us away from rather than to the center of the preoccupations of the time. For Frost cannot embrace the transcendentalism that his sense of nature suggests; but neither does he have the so much wilder sense of nature that our latest nature philosophy requires. Our nature philosophy has been made not only by Darwin but by Freud and Frazer. It connects not only man's body but his mind and culture to the primeval ooze; and you cannot convey that sense of nature in poems about the cultivated countryside of England or New England. [331]

ṹ JOHN F. LYNEN[16]

That Frost's dominant mode is pastoral may at first seem doubtful, because the conventions so characteristic of this genre are not to be found in his verse. The unhappy shepherd, the fair shepherdess, the wandering flock, the daisies and violets, the greensward dance, the flowery wreath and oaten pipe represent a cluster of motifs which can be traced in the tradition from Theocritus to Pope and beyond in the nineteenth century. So prominent are the conventions that one may suppose they are an essential element of pastoral form. Part of the pleasure which the old pastorals offer is that of recognizing the familiar images as they appear, just as another part consists in noting how skillfully the poet handles the traditional devices of dialogue, singing contest, and lament. [13]

. . . The conventions are not the true basis of pastoral, but an outgrowth of something deeper and more fundamental. Pas-

[16] From *The Pastoral Art of Robert Frost*, New Haven: Yale University, 1960, pp. 13-27.

toralism requires an established myth of the rural world, and the conventions gradually developed through tradition belong to the myth of Arcadia. They are formalized symbols whose function is to evoke an imaginative vision of this world. But Arcadia is not the only version of rural life, and it is possible for a poet to write true pastorals within the context of some other mythic world. . . . [14]

Frost's method as pastoral poet is nicely illustrated by one of his most familiar lyrics, "The Pasture." This poem is of particular interest in that the poet has for many years used it as the epigraph for editions of his collected verse, a fact which suggests that he regards it as a symbol of the kind of poetry he writes. "The Pasture" may at first appear very simple indeed, since the materials of which it is composed are so slight. It seems merely to describe a few casual details of farm life which the poet sees in going about his tasks. But as in "Stopping by Woods," the bits of description somehow cohere to form a pattern which expresses a much broader meaning than is overtly stated. [21] It is important to note that the poem is an invitation: the poet invites someone, perhaps a person he loves, perhaps just a friend, to come with him and see the glimpses of delicate beauty to be found in the pasture. The implication is that the person invited knows little of such things. More important, he will have to be initiated into the special way of looking at them which makes them precious and meaningful. The leaves floating in the pasture spring, the little calf, so young it totters when its mother licks it, have the simplicity and innocence of pristine reality, and the poem implies that the average person, like the person invited, could not see the beauty in such natural, everyday things without the poet as guide. To appreciate these, he will have to abandon knowledge as the great world understands it and learn to adopt the poet's special way of seeing.

The poet's invitation is really to a kind of vision, and this vision is to be understood through its implicit difference from the common view of reality. But the invitation is also to a place, the pasture itself, for only within the humble, out-of-the-way rural world is this special mode of perception possible. The pasture, then, is both the subject of the vision and its perspective; the mode of perception is embodied in the images themselves.

For all its sweetness the poem is not tainted by sentimentality, because while it describes the charming aspects of the pasture, it is concerned less with beauty for its own sake than with the organic wholeness which makes this beauty meaningful. Frost's theme here is the coherence of the rural scene, the unity between objects and thought, between man's work—the speaker of the poem must clean the spring and fetch the young calf—and his aesthetic experience. This unity raises the world of the pasture above [22] other realms of human life by showing it as an ordered world where the significance of things is simple and apparent. This is manifest in the symbols themselves: the spring and the calf represent the source, the simple, pure, innocent beginnings of things.

Yet the special value of this world is paradoxical in that the pasture embodies a humble and naive level of being. The reader is to admire the pasture as a world better than his own because it is more natural, more neatly organized, and more meaningful, but he is also aware that it is a plane of existence inferior in many respects to that on which he lives. The contrast between the country and the town which we have noted in pastoral is clearly the essential element in the design of this poem. By making the rural scene remote from ordinary life and by implying that to understand it we must learn to adopt its special perspective, Frost establishes a comparison between the pasture and the outside world. It is from this implied comparison that the poem's elusive symbolism grows. The calf and the pasture spring emerge as symbols because they exist within a world which is viewed in its relation to other places and other modes of experience.

A symbolism created by the sustained contrast of pastoral has its being in the medium of analogy. This explains why in Frost's poetry metaphor is not a dominant element. Of course, Frost uses metaphor frequently and with great effect—at times, even, in a manner quite close to that of metaphysical poetry. But it is a device or figure of speech—it does not, as in Blake, Shelley, or Stevens, supply the essential pattern of thought; and this is so because the mode of thinking metaphor involves is different from that of pastoral. Metaphor establishes an identity between diverse things, while the pastoralist's technique is to keep the image and the thing it resembles separate so [23] that they may be compared.[4] The result is that pastoralism favors an analogical form, a fact illustrated by its persistent tendency toward allegory— that is, extended analogy. . . . [24]

The broad and generalized symbolism characteristic of pastoral results from the fact that the pastoral analogy is implied, rather than stated. While the pastoral poet deals with the great world as well as the rural, he does so indirectly. What he actually portrays is country life. The area extending beyond the limits of his Arcadia serves as a background against which the rural subject is seen in clear silhouette; and precisely because this larger world is never explicitly defined, the rustic scene can represent many other levels of being. Such use of analogy makes the difficulty of interpreting Frost's poetry understandable; it explains why his symbolism, though strongly felt, is always hard to tie down to specific referents. The scenes he portrays do not point toward particular things in other contexts, but rather represent whole classes of experience and types of things. We see this immediately when we attempt to specify what such images as the woods filled with snow in "Stopping by Woods" or the newborn calf in "The Pasture" symbolize. We can say that the woods represent a kind of temptation to indulge the imagination and that the calf suggests birth, fertility, and natural innocence, but beyond this one cannot safely go. In other words, we can delimit the general area of meaning behind the symbol, but this area contains an indefinite number of referents, none of which can be chosen as *the* right one. . . . [25]

Frost's imagery is certainly no less distinct and particular than that of other contemporary poets, but the implied analogy of pastoral through which he works does not create a symbolism as precise in its reference as that of more typical modern poetry. In Eliot's "Sweeney Among the Nightingales," for example, one finds a use of symbols quite different from that we have noted in "The Pasture." Eliot's poem, like Frost's, is based upon the

---

4. Nowadays, there is a tendency to regard the difference between metaphor and simile as unimportant. Often metaphor is used to designate both. If we regard metaphor and simile merely as figures of speech the distinction may not seem important, but each represents a particular kind of poetic structure. In terms of an entire poem, the difference between metaphoric thought and that involved in simile is crucial.

analogy between two distinct levels of being, but here both are stated. Sweeney and his milieu, the bordello or cheap eating [26] house where the hero finds himself surrounded by prostitutes and rather dangerous low-life criminals, comprise the main subject, but its meaning is revealed by comparison with Agamemnon and the whole context of the house of Atreus myth. The elements of Sweeney's story have specific reference to the elements of the myth, Sweeney to Agamemnon, the prostitutes who conspire against him to Clytemnestra, and so forth. Of course, the meaning of Eliot's symbols extends beyond these mythic parallels, but nevertheless the symbolism has a quality of exactitude because the two levels compared are both presented. Frost, by leaving one side of his analogy to implication, achieves a symbolism which appears to be far less precise.

His poetry, however, has its own kind of precision. While the referents of his symbols are not specified, the *area* within which referents are to be found is strictly delimited. While in Eliot the symbol most often has some terminus (though this may be very distant indeed from the symbol itself), and the meaning vibrates between the two like an electric current between two poles, in Frost the symbol, presented quite casually as an image, opens outward upon a vista of meaning. The vista does not have any definite terminus and in the farthest distance fades into vague areas of suggestion. What is definite is the *line* of vision, the direction. [27]

❦ BIBLIOGRAPHY

❧❧❧❧❧❧❧❧❧❧❧❧❧❧❧❧❧❧

Frost's Poetry

A Boy's Will, London: Nutt, 1913; New York: Holt, 1915.

North of Boston, London: Nutt, 1914; New York: Holt, 1914.

Mountain Interval, New York: Holt, 1916.

New Hampshire: A Poem with Notes and Grace Notes, New York: Holt, 1923.

Selected Poems, New York: Holt, 1923; revised and enlarged in 1928 and 1934.

West-running Brook, New York: Holt, 1928.

Collected Poems, New York: Holt, 1930; reissued in 1939, with Frost's prose preface, "The Figure a Poem Makes."

A Further Range, New York: Holt, 1936.

Selected Poems, London: Cape, 1936; includes introductory essays by W. H. Auden, C. Day Lewis, Paul Engle, and Edwin Muir.

A Witness Tree, New York: Holt, 1942.

A Masque of Reason, New York: Holt, 1945.

The Poems of Robert Frost, New York: Modern Library, 1946; includes Frost's prose preface, "The Constant Symbol."

Steeple Bush, New York: Holt, 1947.

A Masque of Mercy, New York: Holt, 1947.

Complete Poems, New York: Holt, 1949; includes "The Figure a Poem Makes."

Books on Robert Frost

Clymer, W. B. and Charles R. Green, *Robert Frost: A Bibliography*, Amherst, Mass.: The Jones Library, 1937.

Coffin, Robert P. Tristram, *New Poetry of New England: Frost and Robinson*, Baltimore: Johns Hopkins, 1938.

Cook, Reginald L., *The Dimensions of Robert Frost*, New York: Rinehart, 1958.

Cox, Sidney, *Robert Frost: Original "Ordinary Man,"* New York: Holt, 1929.

———, *A Swinger of Birches: A Portrait of Robert Frost*, New York: New York University, 1957.

Ford, Caroline, *The Less Traveled Road*, Cambridge: Harvard University, 1935.

Lynen, John F., *The Pastoral Art of Robert Frost*, New Haven: Yale University, 1960.

Mertins, Louis and Esther, *The Intervals of Robert Frost: A Critical Bibliography*, Berkeley and Los Angeles: University of California, 1947.

Munson, Gorham B., *Robert Frost: A Study in Sensibility and Good Sense*, New York: Doran, 1927.

Nitchie, George W., *Human Values in the Poetry of Robert Frost*, Durham, N. C.: Duke University, 1960.

Sergeant, Elizabeth Shepley, *Robert Frost: The Trial by Existence*, New York: Holt, Rinehart, Winston, 1960.

Thompson, Lawrance, *Fire and Ice: The Art and Thought of Robert Frost*, New York: Holt, 1942.

———, *Robert Frost*, University of Minnesota Pamphlets on American Writers, No. 2, Minneapolis: University of Minnesota, 1959.

Thornton, Richard, ed., *Recognition of Robert Frost*, New York: Holt, 1937.

Articles and Comments

Baker, Carlos, "Frost on the Pumpkin," *Georgia Review*, XI (Summer 1957), 117-131.

Beach, Joseph Warren, "Robert Frost," *Yale Review*, XLIII (December 1953), 204-217.

Bowra, C. M., "Reassessments: Robert Frost," *Adelphi*, XXVII (November 1950), 46-64.

Breit, Harvey, "Talk with Robert Frost," *New York Times Book Review* (November 27, 1949), p. 20.

Brooks, Cleanth and Robert Penn Warren, *Understanding Poetry*, rev. ed., New York: Holt, 1951.

Chatman, Seymour, "Robert Frost's 'Mowing': An Inquiry into Prosodic Structure," *Kenyon Review*, XVIII (Summer 1956), 421-438.

Ciardi, John, "Robert Frost, Master Conversationalist at Work," *Saturday Review*, XLII (March 21, 1959), 17-20.

Coffin, Robert P. Tristram, untitled review of *Fire and Ice*, *American Literature*, XIV (January 1943), 435-440.

Cook, Reginald L., "Notes on Frost the Lecturer," *Quarterly Journal of Speech*, XLII (April 1956), 127-132.

———, "Poet in the Mountains," *Western Review*, XI (Spring 1947), 175-181.

Cox, James M., "Robert Frost and the Edge of the Clearing," *Virginia Quarterly Review*, XXXV (Winter 1959), 73-88.

Cox, Sidney, "The Sincerity of Robert Frost," *New Republic*, XII (August 25, 1917), 109-111.

Deen, Rosemary F., "The Voices of Robert Frost," *Commonweal*, LXIX (February 20, 1959), 542-544.

de Voto, Bernard, "The Critics and Robert Frost," *Saturday Review of Literature*, XVII (January 1, 1938), 3-4, 14-15.

Donoghue, Denis, "The Limitations of Robert Frost," *Twentieth Century*, CLXVI (July 1959), 13-22.

Frost, Robert, Introduction to Edwin Arlington Robinson, *King Jasper*, New York: Macmillan, 1935.

———, "Maturity No Object," introduction to *New Poets of England and America*, ed. Donald Hall *et al.*, New York: Meridian, 1957.

———, "On Emerson," *Daedalus*, LXXXVIII (Fall 1959), 712-718.

———, "Poetry and School," *Atlantic Monthly*, CLXXXVII (June 1951), 30-31.

———, "A Poet, Too, Must Learn the Magic Way of Poetry," *New York Times Book Review* (March 21, 1954), p. 1.

———, Reginald Cook, and J. Isaacs, "Thoreau's Walden," *Listener*, LII (August 26, 1954), 319-320.

Garnett, Edward, "A New American Poet," *Atlantic Monthly*, CXVI (August 1915), 214-221.

Holmes, John, "Close-up of an American Poet at 75," *New York Times Magazine* (March 26, 1950), 12, 72-73, 75-77.

Jarrell, Randall, *Poetry and the Age*, New York: Alfred A. Knopf, Inc., 1955.

Lowell, Amy, *Tendencies in Modern American Poetry*, New York: Macmillan, 1917.

McLaughlin, Charles A., "Two Views of Poetic Unity," *University of Kansas City Review*, XXII (Summer 1956), 309-316.

Monroe, Harriet, *Poets and Their Art*, New York: Macmillan, 1926.

Montgomery, Marion, "Robert Frost and His Use of Barriers: Man vs. Nature towards God," *South Atlantic Quarterly*, LVII (Summer 1958), 339-353.

Mulder, William, "Freedom and Form: Robert Frost's Double Discipline," *South Atlantic Quarterly*, LIV (July 1955), 386-393.

Munford, Howard, "Frost's 'The Subverted Flower,'" *Explicator*, XVII (January 1959), item 31.

Napier, John T., "A Momentary Stay Against Confusion," *Virginia Quarterly Review*, XXXIII (Summer 1957), 378-394.

Newdick, Robert S., "Robert Frost and the Dramatic," *New England Quarterly*, X (June 1937), 262-269.

———, "Robert Frost and the Sound of Sense," *American Literature*, IX (November 1937), 289-300.

O'Donnell, William G., "Robert Frost and New England," *Yale Review*, XXXVII (Summer 1948), 698-712.

Ogilvie, John T., "From Woods to Stars: A Pattern of Imagery in Robert Frost's Poetry," *South Atlantic Quarterly*, LVIII (Winter 1959), 64-76.

Ornstein, Robert, "Frost's 'Come In,'" *Explicator*, XV (June 1957), item 61.

Perrine, Lawrence, "Frost's 'Neither Out Far Nor In Deep,'" *Explicator*, VII (April 1949), item 46.

————, *Sound and Sense*, New York: Harcourt, Brace, 1956.

Pound, Ezra, *Literary Essays*, New York: New Directions, 1954.

Rukeyser, Muriel, "In a Speaking Voice," *Poetry*, LIV (July 1939), 218-224.

Ryan, Alvan S., "Frost and Emerson: Voice and Vision," *Massachusetts Review*, I (October 1959), 5-23.

Scott, Wilbur S., "Frost's 'To Earthward,'" *Explicator*, XVI (January 1958), item 23.

Scott, Winfield Townley, "Frost's Seventh Book," *Poetry*, LX (June 1942), 146-149.

Stallman, R. W., "The Position of Poetry Today," *English Journal*, XLVI (May 1957), 241-251.

Stauffer, Donald B., "Frost's 'The Subverted Flower,'" *Explicator*, XV (March 1957), item 38.

Thompson, Lawrance, "A Native to the Grain of the American Idiom," *Saturday Review*, XLII (March 21, 1959), 21, 55-56.

Thorp, Willard, "The New Poetry," *Literary History of the United States*, ed. Robert E. Spiller *et al.*, New York: Macmillan, 1949, II, 1189-1196.

Untermeyer, Louis, *From Another World*, New York: Harcourt, 1939.

————, "Our Singing Faith," *Saturday Review of Literature*, VII (January 17, 1931), 529-530.

————, *The Road Not Taken*, New York: Holt, 1951.

Van Doren, Mark, "The Permanence of Robert Frost," *American Scholar*, V (Spring 1936), 190-198.

————, "Robert Frost's America," *Atlantic Monthly*, CLXXXVII (June 1951), 32-34.

Waggoner, Hyatt Howe, *The Heel of Elohim*, Norman: University of Oklahoma, 1950.

————, "The Humanistic Idealism of Robert Frost," *American Literature*, XIII (November 1941), 207-223.

Walcutt, Charles Child, "Interpreting the Symbol," *College English*, XIV (May 1953), 446-454.

Warren, Robert Penn, *Selected Essays*, New York: Random House, 1958.

Watts, Harold H., "Robert Frost and the Interrupted Dialogue," *American Literature*, XXVII (March 1955), 69-87.

Wells, Henry W., *The American Way of Poetry*, New York: Columbia University, 1943.

Whicher, George F., "Out for Stars," *Atlantic Monthly*, CLXXI (May 1943), 64-67.

Whipple, T. K., *Spokesmen*, New York: Appleton, 1928.

❦ TOPICS FOR PAPERS

✤✤✤✤✤✤✤✤✤✤✤✤✤✤✤✤✤✤✤✤

Short Papers

Two types of topics follow—research and critical—which are designed to be developed from the pamphlet alone. The research topics offer an opportunity for preliminary exercises in research techniques.

1. Does there seem to be general agreement among Cook, Cowley, and Thompson about the character of the narrator in "Two Tramps in Mud Time"?

2. In what ways would you consider "Come In" a companion poem to "Stopping by Woods on a Snowy Evening"?

* 3. What do Lowell, Untermeyer, and Benét imply about the character of Frost as a person?

4. Though "Home Burial" has many of the characteristics of a regional poem, can a case be made for its significance in other than regional terms?

5. What relationships of the poet to nature are suggested by Thompson, Ciardi, and Dabbs?

6. Do you think Frost's attitude toward mankind in "Neither Out Far Nor In Deep" is cynical or sympathetic?

7. How significant to his poetry does Frost's New England background seem to Morton, Wheelwright, and Hicks?

8. Do you see any special qualities of tone, language, and structure in "A Soldier" that distinguish it from the other poems in the pamphlet?

9. What relationships do Benét and Jarrell see between Frost the man and his poetry?

10. Frost makes a statement about the world in "A Drumlin Woodchuck." What is the effect of his doing so from the point of view of a woodchuck?

11. How well do Pound, Benét, and Winters agree on the quality of Frost's language?

12. Contrast Brooks and Schneider in their discussions of Frost's uniting the realistic and the poetic.

13. What is the contribution of the metaphorical language to the tone and meaning of "The Subverted Flower"?

14. Compare Ciardi's description of the making of "Stopping by Woods on a Snowy Evening" with Frost's own comments on the making of it.

15. Compare the assumptions about the nature and function of poetry that lie behind the judgments of Frost's poetry by Fitts, Wheelwright, and Hicks.

Long Papers

The research and critical topics that follow can be developed from the pamphlet alone. Several of them, however, have additional references, so that if the teacher desires, the student may use the pamphlet in conjunction with library research. See the Bibliography for full descriptions of these references.

1. Considering both the reviews and general criticism, do you discern any shift over a period of time in what seem to the critics to be the most praiseworthy qualities of Frost's poetry?

2. Present a case for Frost as either an optimist or a pessimist. Draw upon Frost's poetry and the criticism to support your view. (Donoghue, Holmes, Thompson in the *Saturday Review*, Untermeyer in the *Saturday Review*.)

3. Discuss Frost's humor, or his irony, in the poems in the pamphlet.

4. Insofar as Frost is thought by his critics to be a regional poet, what are the characteristics of his poetry by which they define him as one? (Coffin in *New Poetry of New England*, Lowell, Monroe, O'Donnell, Whipple.)

5. In what differing persons does Frost appear in the several poems in the pamphlet? Write a paper on one or more of these persons, showing how they contribute to the qualities of the poems.

6. Distinguish the different views of the critics on Frost's relationship to society. Make a case from the poems in the pamphlet for the one that seems to you to be most satisfactory.

7. Do Frost's critics generally assume that there is a relationship between the character of the man and the character of his poetry? To what extent do they praise or condemn the poetry by praising or condemning the man? (Beach, Sidney Cox in the *New Republic*, Ogilvie, Perrine in *Explicator*.)

8. Do the didactic or moral elements in the poems in the pamphlet seem consistent with each other? Do they offer a clear, coherent outlook?

9. To what extent do the critics agree about the sort of audience to which Frost chiefly appeals? Do they count themselves as members of that audience?

10. What are the qualities of Frost's language that critics note? Are the critics in general agreement? What assumptions about the proper language of poetry lie behind their remarks? (Deen, Garnett, Newdick in *American Literature*, Rukeyser, W. T. Scott.)

11. Analyze the extent to which the dominant metaphor in "To Earthward," "A Soldier," and "The Subverted Flower" governs the development and meaning of the poem.

12. Frost's relationship to nature is a major strain in the criticism on him. Distinguish between the different views of that relationship. Support the view that seems to you to be most satisfactory with a discussion of the poems in the pamphlet. (Montgomery, Waggoner, Watts, Wells.)

13. Compare the several interpretations of "Stopping by Woods on a Snowy Evening" given throughout the pamphlet. To what extent do they differ? How adequate do the arguments seem? What do the differences in interpretation suggest about the nature of the poem or the nature of poetry?

14. Lionel Trilling says: "my Frost is not the Frost I seem to perceive existing in the minds of so many of his admirers." On the basis of the material in the pamphlet, how valid does his assertion seem to be? (Baker, Beach, Holmes, Van Doren in the *Atlantic Monthly*.)

15. In their general discussion of Frost, Unger and O'Connor mention a "recurring pattern of development" in his poems. Examine some of the poems in the pamphlet (other than "Stopping by Woods on a Snowy Evening" and "Two Tramps in Mud Time") for this pattern.

16. With whom among the commentators on "Stopping by

Woods on a Snowy Evening" does Frost implicitly align himself in his discussion of the breakdown of metaphor in "Education by Poetry"?

17. Write a paper on the theme of renunciation as it is discussed by several of the critics and as it appears in several of the poems in the pamphlet. (James Cox, Waggoner, Warren, Whicher.)

18. The line between analysis and evaluation is not always clearly drawn by critics. Take four or five criticisms of Frost and distinguish sharply between the characteristics they attribute to his poetry and the merits they attach to the characteristics.

19. Do Frost, in his comments on writing poetry, and his critics, in their comments, seem to be talking about the same things? Do they emphasize the same concerns, the same values? (Ciardi, Frost in the *Atlantic Monthly*, Mulder.)

20. The poems in the pamphlet present a variety of moods and tones. Do you discern an underlying unity?